Deep Learning from Scratch

From Basics to Building Real Neural Networks with Keras. Illustrated Introduction for Absolute Beginners.

Artem Kovera

Deep Learning from Scratch: From Basics to Building Real Neural Networks with Keras. Illustrated Introduction for Beginners.

ISBN 9781731175625

Contents

Part I Deep Learning Theory Made Easy to Understand

Introduction to machine learning and deep learning

As opposed to biological beings, computers are often viewed as entities that can perform only some explicit and rigid rules, known as algorithms, designed by humans. So, from this point of view, computers can't really adapt the processes they execute to changing environments without human interventions. And it's partly true. But computers can also learn and adapt their behavior to some degree. This remarkable capability of digital machines arises due to a general category of different approaches known as *machine learning*.

In a machine learning framework, we also have an algorithm designed by humans in the first place. But this is a special algorithm that can learn. A simplified general framework for machine learning can be described as follows. A machine learning algorithm is given some training data. After training on this data, the algorithm produces a model. Then, we can give new data to this model, on which the model can makes predictions:

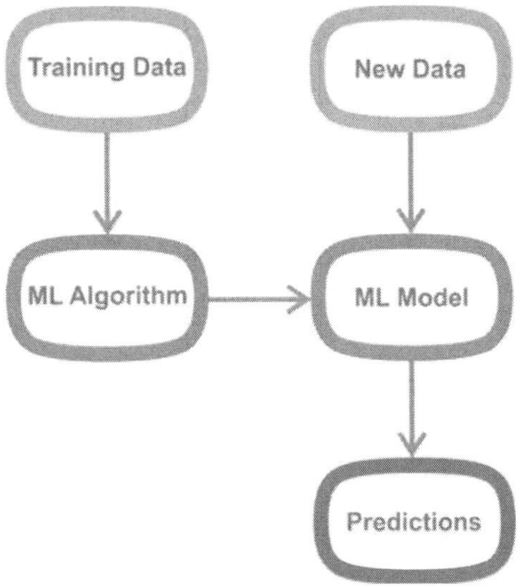

In this framework, a machine learning algorithm can be viewed as a process that produces other sets of instructions (other algorithms) for a computer.

For many problems, a machine learning framework boils down to a surprisingly simple procedure: computing the outputs of a given function on new inputs, given some known outputs for other inputs. If you're familiar with statistics, it can be viewed as a regression problem. At a first glance, figuring out outputs of a function on new inputs can be viewed as a very simple problem. But keep in mind that the functions can be extremely complicated and have an enormous number of variables and we need to learn these functions given only a limited number of input-output matches.

For instance, think about the brain. The brain receives the input from the sensory organs and other body parts and sends new signals to the rest of the body. Apparently, this is an extraordinary complex multidimensional function. If someday machines learn this function and can implement it, we will have artificial general intelligence. I wrote about that stuff in my previous little book *How to Create Machine Superintelligence*. By the way, the human brain is believed to be the most complex structure in the universe. In theory, any process can be viewed as a function. We'll get to it shortly.

Obviously, the more input-output matches we know, the more accurate our predictions can be. This is why having a sufficient amount of training data is crucially important for all machine learning tasks. The quality of the data is also extremely important. The form in which we give the data to a computer also matters significantly. First of all, every data has to be converted to numbers.

In many situations, we can represent a dataset in a tabular form. For example, here is a table of the first five data points from the famous iris dataset:

	sepal length (cm)	sepal width (cm)	petal length (cm)	petal width (cm)
0	5.1	3.5	1.4	0.2
1	4.9	3.0	1.4	0.2
2	4.7	3.2	1.3	0.2
3	4.6	3.1	1.5	0.2
4	5.0	3.6	1.4	0.2

In this table, each row (0, 1, 2, 3, 4) represents a *data point* (also known as *sample* or *training example*), and each column ('sepal length (cm)', 'sepal width (cm)', etc) represents an entity also with several different names: *feature, variable, dimension,* or *attribute*. We can see that we have four features in this dataset.

However, in many other tasks, we have much more features and those features are not usually represented in a tabular form.

We often need to normalize our data before throwing them into an ML algorithm. Normalization means converting different features into the same range of values. Without normalization, features with bigger ranges of values would be more significant than other features, and this often significantly impacts training in a negative way. But before applying a machine learning algorithm, we should also know to what type of probability distribution the training data belong in order to normalize the data correctly. Most often, the data belong to the normal distribution, which we'll discuss in the next chapter.

There is a famous quote by the great ancient Greek mathematician and engineer Archimedes of Syracuse: "Give me a place to stand, and I shall move the world". Maybe we can a little bit paraphrase this expression: give data scientists appropriate ML algorithms, enough training data, and computational resources, and they can do virtually everything. It seems, though, Archimedes was less picky because he only needed a place to stand.

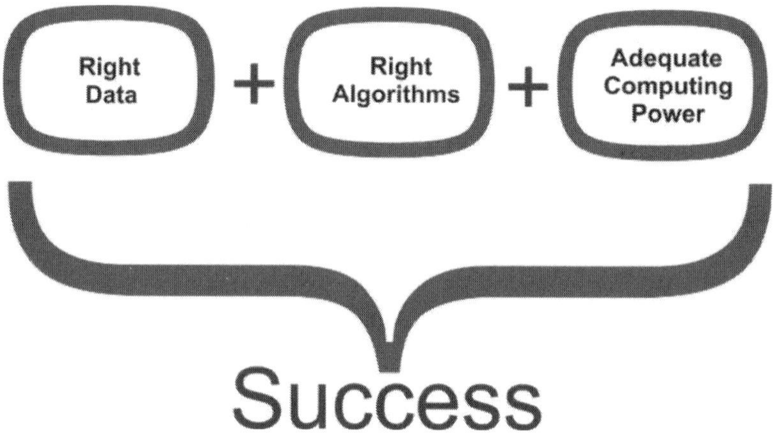

Statistics and machine learning are closely related fields, and both work with data. But machine learning is a more engineering oriented and empirical discipline.

As you probably know, machine learning is part of a broader category of approaches known as *artificial intelligence* (AI). Some researchers think that machine learning is the only possible paradigm from many others to create truly intelligent machines. Now machine learning is the most successful branch of AI. We use different applications of machine learning on a regular basis often without even realizing it.

There are a tremendous number of different machine learning algorithms. But all of these algorithms can be divided into several broad categories: supervised learning, unsupervised learning, and reinforcement learning.

Supervised learning is a type of learning where pieces of training data are labeled with descriptions or values. Supervised learning itself consists of two subcategories: regression and classification. Regression is such a sub-type of supervised learning when input data are labeled with real numbers; whereas classification is a sub-type where labels represent classes. Currently, supervised machine learning gives most practical results in comparison to other types of ML, but it also has a serious disadvantage: data labeling is a tedious task and often requires a lot of work which has to be done by humans.

In the case of unsupervised learning, we do not have any labeled training data, and we need to extract some meaning from this unlabeled data. Broadly speaking, the aim of unsupervised learning is discovering meaningful patterns in datasets. A typical task of unsupervised learning is clustering. Clustering is a process of finding groups of similar objects in datasets.

In reinforcement learning, a machine learning agent or system has a goal or a set of goals. The agent observes its environment and has to decide what actions to take to achieve its goals. The agent gets a numerical reward whenever it chooses the actions that lead to achieving its goals.

Machine learning algorithms can be also divided into two big classes based on the complexity of *data transformations* which occur inside ML algorithms. In this context, data transformations are also called *data representations*.

So, the first class of ML algorithms with respect to a complexity of data representations represents simple (traditional) machine learning algorithms. Such algorithms implement only one or two layers of data representations.

The second class is deep learning. These algorithms can implement many layers of data representations, and this significantly improves their capabilities. But deep learning usually requires significantly more computational resources than traditional ML algorithms. In principle, deep learning can be implemented in several different ways, but the most common type of deep learning is based on using so-called deep neural networks, and this book is all about them. Deep learning can be of different types: supervised, unsupervised, or reinforcement.

Simple machine learning algorithms heavily rely on the features they process. In this case, data scientists often have to extract useful features – if the features haven't been already extracted – from raw data in order to solve the problem they are working on. On the contrary, deep learning is a type of machine learning that can automatically extract useful features or abstractions from raw input data and use these abstractions for data analysis. For example, if we perform image classification by using some simple ML algorithms such as Random Forest, we need to have some features such as the presence of certain patterns in the images and decide which features to choose in the algorithm, but if we applied a deep neural network instead of using a simple ML algorithm, we would simply pass raw pixel values of the images into the network. Oftentimes, working with features manually is an immensely time-consuming process. In addition, feature engineering often requires a considerable amount of domain knowledge about the problem. So, in this respect, deep learning brings a lot of benefits.

However, I should say that even though deep learning can use raw data and automatically extract useful features from them, we still often need to spend a considerable amount of time to prepare appropriate datasets. Having the right data for our deep models is absolutely mandatory. Oftentimes, it's even more important than many modifications to our algorithms we're working with.

When data scientists have numerical data in a tabular form, say like excel sheets, simple machine learning algorithms usually work very well. Because of this, simple machine learning algorithms are still more frequently used in data analysis than deep learning. Clearly, we shouldn't use a bulldozer when we can use a simple tool like a hammer.

Currently, deep learning is mostly applied dealing with image, video, sound, and text formats of data. The achievements of deep learning in these domains are amazing. For example, without deep learning self-driving cars and many other autonomous vehicles wouldn't be possible; machine translation now performed by deep neural networks is much better than other types of machine translation; deep learning has made possible various personal virtual assistants such as Amazon Alexa or Google Now. And this is just a small fraction of deep learning applications. No doubt, deep learning will be even more prevalent in various applications in the near future. For instance, some experts believe that significant amounts of the content on the web will soon be generated by deep neural networks.

The performance of traditional machine learning algorithms usually reaches a plateau at a certain point, regardless of the amount of data available for training. But deep learning models behave differently, and their performance usually always gets better and better with more and more training data. This is another important advantage of deep learning.

However, I should admit that deep neural networks have also some other drawbacks aside from their gargantuan appetite in computational resources. As opposed to some traditional machine learning algorithms, one quite important disadvantage of deep neural networks is that when we have a solution to our problem obtained by a neural network, we cannot really explain why this particular solution has been obtained by this network. Sometimes, neural networks are regarded as black boxes that produce solutions to problems but we can’t really see what’s going on inside them. However, there are some methods that can allow us to do that.

Finally, I should also mention that deep learning and artificial intelligence are very often overhyped in the media. On the internet, for instance, we can find countless popular articles where machine learning algorithms such as neural networks are intensely and unduly anthropomorphized.

Initially, first artificial neural networks had been indeed largely inspired by the structure of biological neural networks. Some later types of artificial neural networks were also loosely inspired by biological neural nets. But the differences between artificial and biological neural networks in the brain are so profound – and so are the differences between their capabilities – that the relationship between artificial and biological neural networks is mostly metaphorical.

Math for deep learning explained to the layman.

Maybe if you've already encountered some literature on deep learning, you've seen a lot of heavy and maybe even arcane looking math formalism in it and maybe that stopped you from reading that literature. I was in the same situation many times. A good understanding of deep learning requires at least a minimum understanding of some mathematical concepts. I'm not a mathematician, but I will try to explain at a conceptual level and as simple as possible some minimal mathematical background for understanding deep learning. In case you're good at math, simply skip this chapter and go straight to the next one.

Functions and derivatives

Probably, the most important mathematical concept that we need in order to understand deep learning is the idea of a function. So, let me explain what matters for deep learning in the domain of mathematical functions.

In mathematics, a function is simply a rule that matches some inputs to some outputs. A function can produce only one output for a single input, and it is important. So, a function can be represented in a tabular form, for example:

input	-2	-1	0	1	2	3
output	-6	-3	0	3	6	9

Inputs are also called arguments. Also, inputs in aggregate are called the domain of a function. The outputs of a function in aggregate are called a range. An output is also often called a dependant variable, and an input is called an independent variable. To avoid any confusion, I will be mostly using the terms output and input throughout this book.

A function can be defined by an equation. For example, in a function which is defined by the equation $y=3x$, x is an independent variable or input, and ***y*** is an output or dependant variable.

It's also a very common notation: ***f(x)=y***, which means a function of ***x*** equals ***y***. Using this notation the function ***y=3x*** can be written as ***f(x)=3x***.

In addition to tabular and algebraic forms, some functions can be represented visually on a graph, for example:

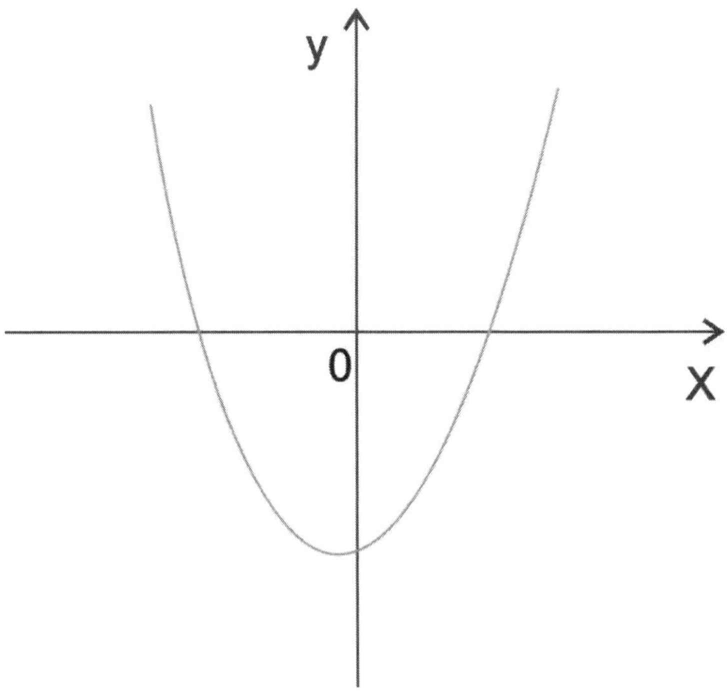

A function can have an arbitrary number of inputs for a single output. Functions with one input per output (for example, $y=3x$ or $y=x^2$) can be plotted on a 2-dimensional graph, with one dimension for the input, and another for the output.

Functions with two inputs for one output can be represented on a 3-dimensional graph. In this case, two dimensions are for the inputs and one for the output, for example:

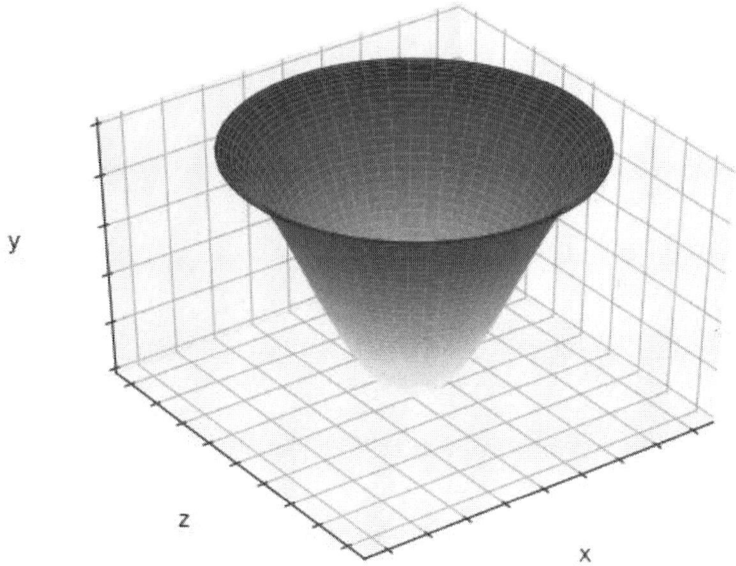

Please note, that we cannot visualize or even envision functions with three or more variables (multivariable functions) – unless we have some mental disorders – as we live in a 3-dimensional world and our biological brains, apparently, have not been evolved to adapt to living in more than 3-dimensional environments. But what we can infer from functions with one or two inputs we can often adopt for multivariable functions. This means we can work algebraically with functions that have more than two dimensions.

Note, if we know a sufficient quantity of input-output matches, we can infer or learn a corresponding rule or a function that has produced these input-output matches. Or we can say, in this case, that we approximate a function.

Functions can be linear or non-linear. One-input linear functions can be depicted by a straight line on a plot. Whereas 2-input ones represent a plane in a 3-dimentional space.

Linear functions with 3 or more variables form a structure called a hyper-plane.

The simplest one-input linear function is simply ***y=x***:

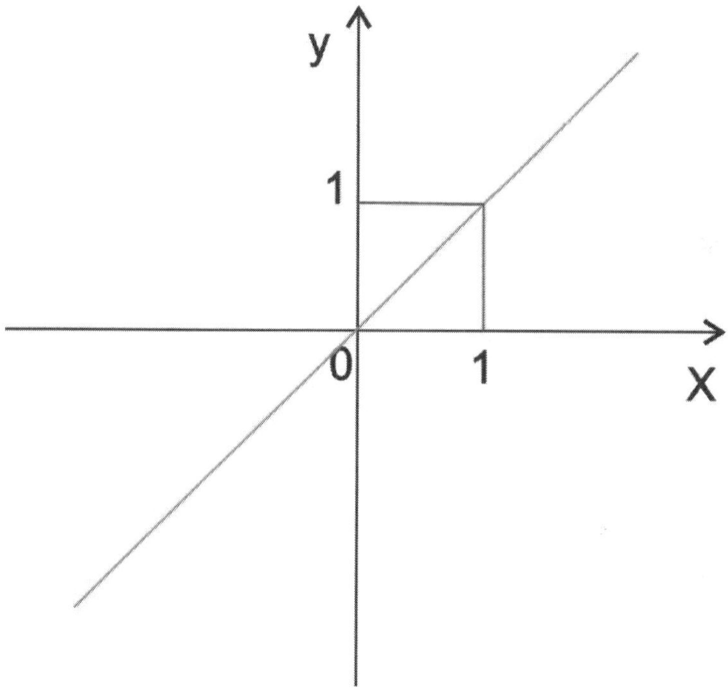

Function can be either continuous or have gaps, like in this example:

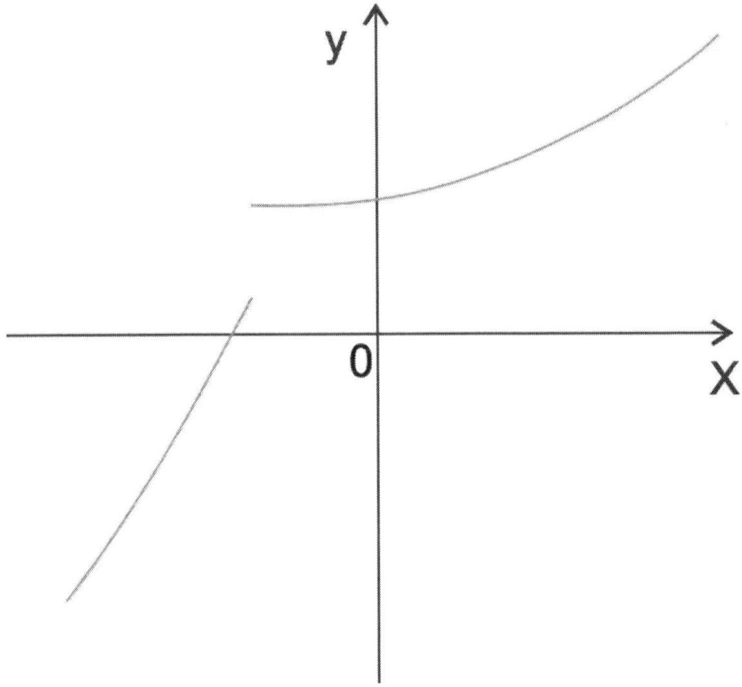

A function can be a composition of other functions. For example, the output of one function may be the input of another one: $y=f_1(f_0(x))$. In this manner, we can compose however many functions we want. Also, composite functions can be denoted by using the "∘" symbol.

For example, the notation for a function ***f*** composed of another function ***g*** can be depicted as

$$(f \circ g)(x) = f(g(x))$$

Building composite functions is the essence of deep learning. Shortly I'll explain in detail why it is.

A function can be increasing, decreasing or constant at a certain point.

The math concept of a *derivative* shows how a function changes at a given point.

A derivative of a function can be viewed as the slope of this function, for example:

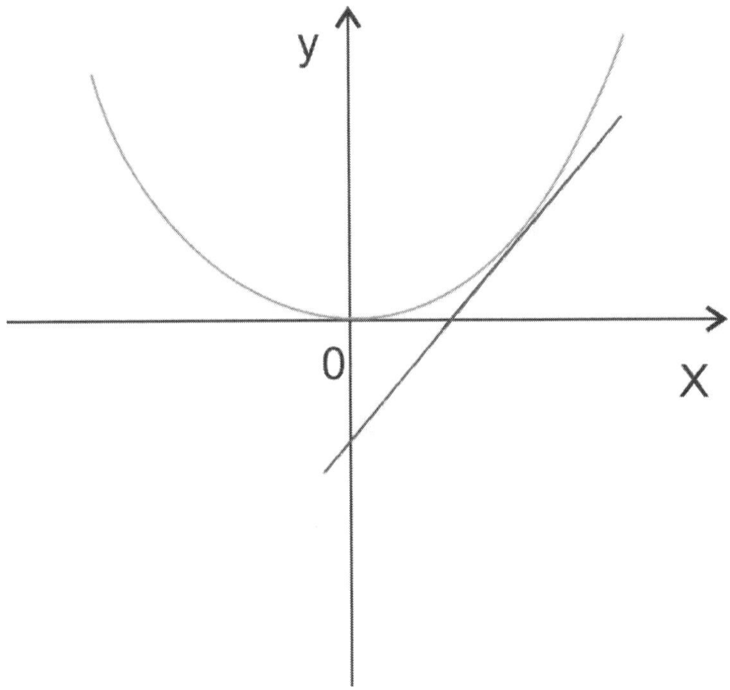

A slope of a linear function is constant and coincides with the function itself. Because of this, derivatives of a linear function are equal and extremely easy to compute.

A derivative can be positive (a function increases), negative (a function decreases), or equal to zero (a function doesn't change).

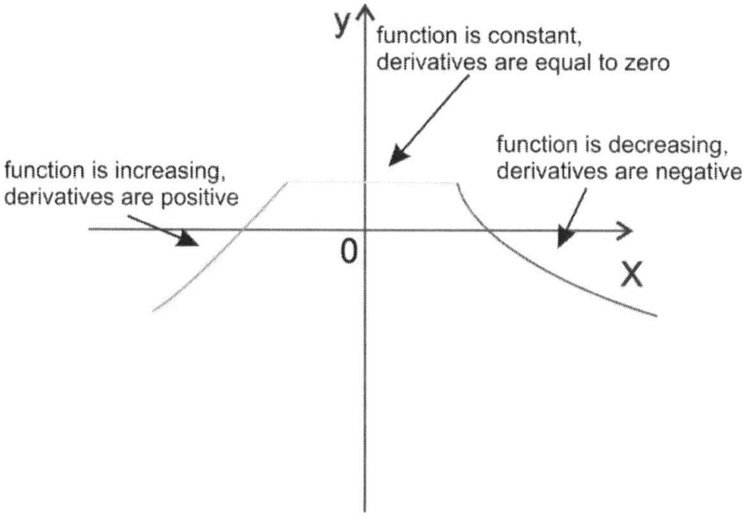

The steeper the graph of a function at a certain point, the greater is the derivative of this function at this point. Conversely, if a graph is very flat at a certain location, the derivatives are close to zero, and this is important in the context of deep learning, and shortly you'll see why.

Also, it is also possible that a derivative cannot be taken at all at some points of a function graph, which means that this function is not differentiable at those locations. Derivatives don't exist at points where a function has gaps or sharp edges.

There are two different notations for dealing with derivatives: Newton's notation and Leibniz's notation.

Newton and Leibniz were two independent co-creators of calculus.

Newton's notation is also known as the prime form. In this notation, a derivative of a function is denoted by putting a prime sign in the right upper corner of a function, for example: ***f'(x)*** or ***g'(x)***.

Leibniz's notation works in a different way. In this notation we use the symbol ***d*** to denote a function. Also, in this notation, we can explicitly specify with respect to which variable we take a derivative of a function. For example, the expression

$$\frac{dy}{dx}$$

means that we take a derivative of ***y*** with respect of **x**. And this is very useful for dealing with composite functions, so this notation is very common in deep learning.

There are some rules for operating with derivatives. I will not explain them all here because the focus of this book is not on calculus. Here I'll just say that, in the context of deep learning, the crucial rule with derivatives is the *chain rule*. According to this rule, a derivative of a composite function equals to a product of derivatives of the functions that form this composite function:

$$f(g(x)) = f'(g(x)) * g'(x)$$

or in Leibniz's notation:

$$\frac{df}{dx} = \frac{df}{dg} * \frac{dg}{dx}$$

The chain rule can be applied for compositions of multiple functions. For example:

$$f(a(g(x))) = f'(a(g(x))) * a'(g(x)) * g'(x)$$

Please note that the term derivative applies for functions having only one independent variable. For functions with more than one variable, the equivalent concept to a derivative is a *gradient*.

A gradient at a point of a function is a vector of *partial derivatives* of this function. By the way, a vector is also an essential mathematical concept to understand deep learning. For now, I'll just say that a vector is a list of numbers.

A partial derivative of a multivariable function is a derivative with respect to one independent variable when the other partial derivatives are held constant. A partial derivative can be thought of as a slope with respect to just one direction for a multivariable function.

The notation for gradients and partial derivatives is different from derivatives. Gradients are denoted by this symbol: ∇(the nabla symbol).

Whereas partial derivatives are denoted by this symbol in Leibniz's notation: ∂, for example:

$$\frac{\partial y}{\partial x}$$

The rules for operating with derivatives can be extrapolated to operating with partial derivatives.

Functions can have minimums and maximums – which are called function extrema (plural for extremum) – both global and local.

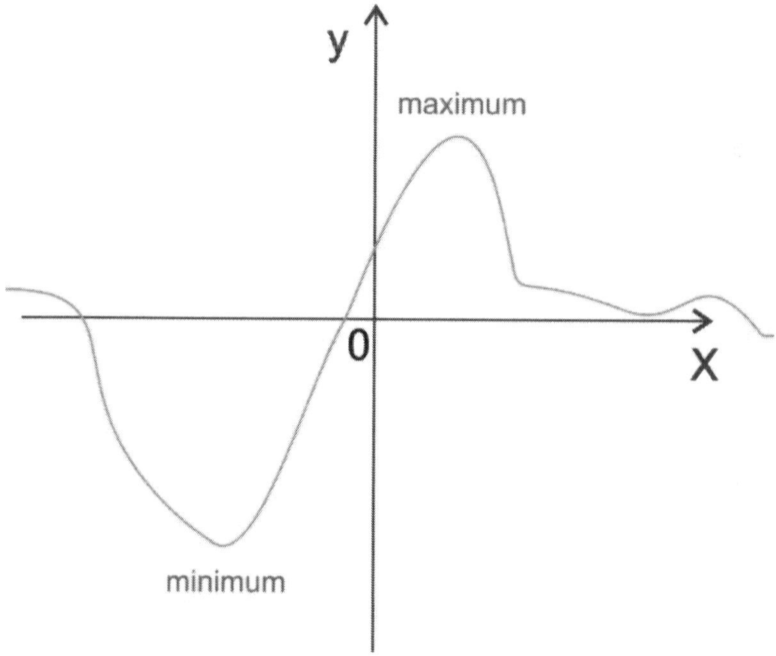

In order to find such function extrema, there is a group of computational methods collectively called *gradient-based optimization*, which lies at the heart of deep learning.

Vectors, matrixes, and tensors

In this section of the book, my goal is not to explain all linear algebra but give you just enough minimum of linear algebra to understand deep neural networks at least at an elementary level.

First of all, we should consider vectors. As I said, a vector is also one of the essential math concepts to understand machine learning and deep learning in particular. A vector is a list of numbers. It can either be in a column or row form:

$$\begin{bmatrix} 7 \\ 8 \\ 9 \\ 6 \end{bmatrix} \qquad \begin{bmatrix} 4 & 7 & 11 & -8 \end{bmatrix}$$

column vector

row vector

Oftentimes, the number of vector components is regarded as the dimensionality of a vector, with one dimension for each component. For example, here is a 5-dimensional vector: [6, 10, 56, 8, 9], and this is a 4-dimensional one: [2, 5, 1, 7]

Another key concept for understanding deep learning is the concept of a matrix. A matrix is just a table of numbers or a stack of a number of vectors combined together:

$$\begin{bmatrix} 8 & 10 & 15 & -2 \\ 11 & 9 & 4 & -3 \\ 3 & 6 & 18 & 44 \end{bmatrix}$$

There is a certain operation called transposition or transpose transformation, denoted by the symbol ***T***. By applying the transpose transformation, we can get a column vector from a row vector and vice versa. It's very simple, for example:

$$[0{,}8 \quad 1{,}5 \quad 0{,}75 \quad 1{,}1]^T = \begin{bmatrix} 0{,}8 \\ 1{,}5 \\ 0{,}75 \\ 1{,}1 \end{bmatrix}$$

$$\begin{bmatrix} 0{,}8 \\ 1{,}5 \\ 0{,}75 \\ 1{,}1 \end{bmatrix}^T = [0{,}8 \quad 1{,}5 \quad 0{,}75 \quad 1{,}1]$$

The transposition transformation can also be applied to matrixes.

We can multiply a vector by a matrix. But we can't multiply a vector by an arbitrary matrix. The dimension of the row vector must be equal to the number of the rows in the matrix, for example:

$$[\,0{,}5 \;\; 1{,}2\,] \times \begin{bmatrix} 2 & 1{,}4 & 1{,}2 \\ 0{,}4 & 1 & 0{,}5 \end{bmatrix}$$

$$=$$

$$[\,(0{,}5\text{x}2)+(1{,}2\text{x}0{,}4) \quad (0{,}5\text{x}1{,}4)+(1{,}2\text{x}1) \quad (0{,}5\text{x}1{,}2)+(1{,}2\text{x}0{,}5)\,]$$

$$=$$

$$[\,1{,}48 \;\; 1{,}9 \;\; 1{,}2\,]$$

So, as a result of this vector-matrix multiplication, we get a new row vector.

Also, a matrix can be multiplied by another matrix.

We can also compute a *dot product* between two vectors with equal dimensions. A dot product is a scalar (a single number).

For example, let's take a dot product of two 3-dimensional vectors: *a* [a_1, a_2, a_3] and *b* [b_1, b_2, b_3]:

Dot product of *a* and *b* = $a_1b_1 + a_2b_2 + a_3b_3$

For one more example, let's compute a dot product of two 4-dimensional vectors: *c* [2, 4, 1, 2] and *d* [3, 1, 2, 1]:

Dot product of c and d = 2x3 + 4x1 + 1x2 + 2x1 = 14

I should also point out that a function can be applied to each element of a vector or matrix. For example, if we apply the function $y=x^2$ to the elements of the vector [2, 3, 4, 5], the output will be [4, 9, 16, 25]. As you can see, we've squared each component of this vector.

We also need a category called *tensor*. A tensor is a matrix with more than 2 dimensions. A 3-dimensional tensor can be easily visualized. A tensor can have an arbitrary number of dimensions. In tensors, a dimension is also called an *axis*.

However, matrixes, vectors, and even scalars can also be considered tensors, and this is usually the case in the context of deep learning. So, with this respect, a matrix is a 2-dimensional tensor, a vector is a 1-dimensional tensor, and a scalar – which is simply a single number – is a tensor with zero dimensions. The number of tensor dimensions is also called *rank*.

But please don't confuse tensor dimensions with vector dimensions.

In the Python programming language, which we will be using in the second part of this book, there is a special library called NumPy for dealing with tensors. In this library, tensors are called Numpy arrays. And this is the major data type we'll be working with.

Probability distributions

The last topic I want to touch on in this chapter about the math for deep learning is *probability distributions* and some related to it concepts.

Probability distribution is basically a function whose outputs are distributed with a certain probability. For example, we can have a distribution that produces only two outputs: 1 and 0 with the same probability (50%). This distribution belongs to discrete distributions because its output is discrete.

There are also continuous distributions. A continuous distribution is a distribution whose outcomes can have values in a continuous range i.e. real numbers.

There are many types of probability distributions both discrete and continuous. For doing data analysis, it's very important to be able to determine the type of the probability distribution of the data being analyzed. There are also other instances where understanding certain probability distributions comes in handy for doing different types of data analysis. In this book, I'll explain just one of many possible probability distributions. This is the *Gaussian distribution*.

The Gaussian distribution, also known as the *normal distribution* is a very common type of continuous distributions. It is called normal because when the number of observations is sufficiently large, the values of the outcomes become normally distributed. Many processes in the real physical world can be viewed as nearly normal distributions.

If we have one-dimensional space, the normal distribution can be represented as a bell curve. The curve is taller in the middle.

We need only two parameters to define the Gaussian distribution: a mean and standard deviation. The normal distribution is average about its mean.

There is a special type of the normal distribution called *standard normal distribution*. It's a normal distribution with a mean of 0 and a standard deviation of 1.

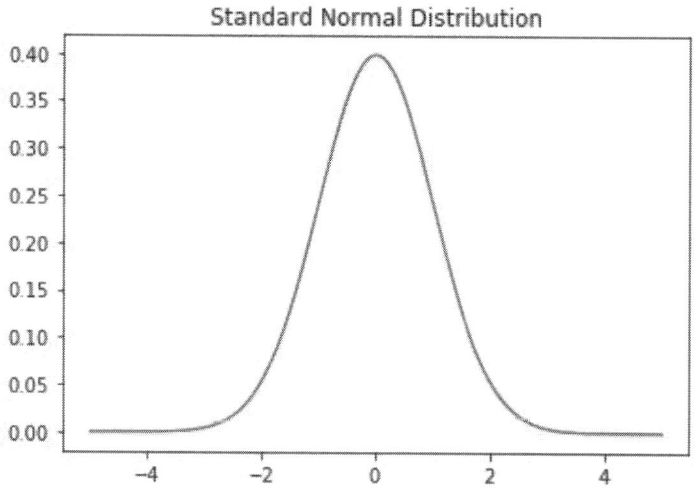

The concept of the *standard deviation* is extremely important for data analytics. The standard deviation shows the variability of data. For example, these two small datasets:

10	11	9	10	10	11	10	9

100	0	-20	30	-2	-3	-26	1

both have the same mean, which is 10, but they are not very similar to each other because the standard deviation of the second set is much higher.

The formula for the standard deviation is

$$s = \sqrt{\frac{\sum_{i=1}^{N}(x_i - \mu)^2}{N-1}},$$

where

s – standard deviation;

N – the number of samples;

μ – mean;

x_i – values of samples

The standard deviation determines the shape of the Gaussian distribution curve. If the standard deviation is smaller, the bell of the curve is narrower and taller.

How neural networks work: a general overview

As I mentioned in the first chapter, the most common way for building deep learning models is using deep neural networks.

First artificial neural networks were called perceptrons. Perceptrons do not belong to deep neural networks, but we should also discuss them briefly before diving into the deep waters of deep learning.

The structure of a typical perceptron is:

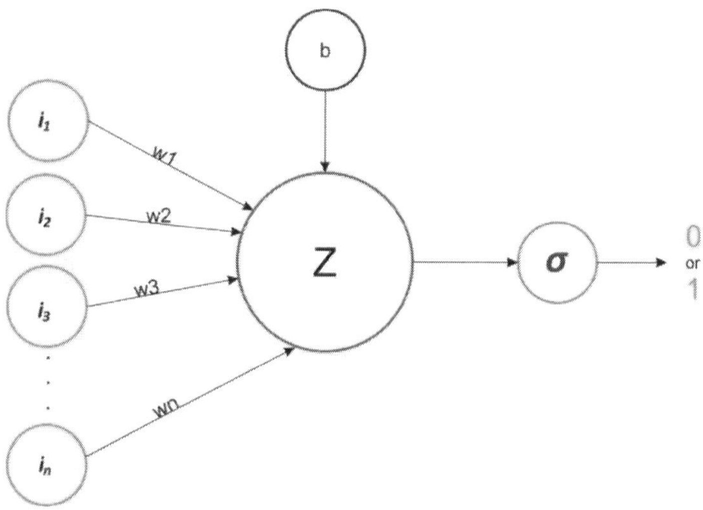

In a perceptron, inputs (***i***) are multiplied by weights (***w***) and summed up. Also, there is an entity called *bias* (***b***) or an activation parameter, which is also added to the sum (***Z***) of the inputs multiplied by the weights. A bias gives additional flexibility to a perceptron's learning capabilities, although a perceptron can work without it. Then the sum ***Z*** goes through a step function (***σ***). This function converts ***Z*** to 1 if ***Z*** is greater than a certain threshold; otherwise ***σ*** converts ***Z*** to 0.

Usually, the initial values of weights in a perceptron are set to random numbers from a standard normal distribution. In this case, the training process of a perceptron usually takes fewer iterations and therefore is faster.

During training, a perceptron adjusts the values of its weights, using the following algorithm:

1. Choose a training sample;

2. If the predicted output for this sample matches its label, do nothing;

3. If the perceptron predicts a 0 but it should have predicted a 1, add the input vector to the weight vector;

4. If the perceptron predicts a 1 but it should have predicted a 0, subtract the input vector from the weight vector.

The biggest limitation of perceptrons is that they can learn only linear functions.

For example, perceptrons can separate data points only by a straight line in classification tasks. Sometimes it works:

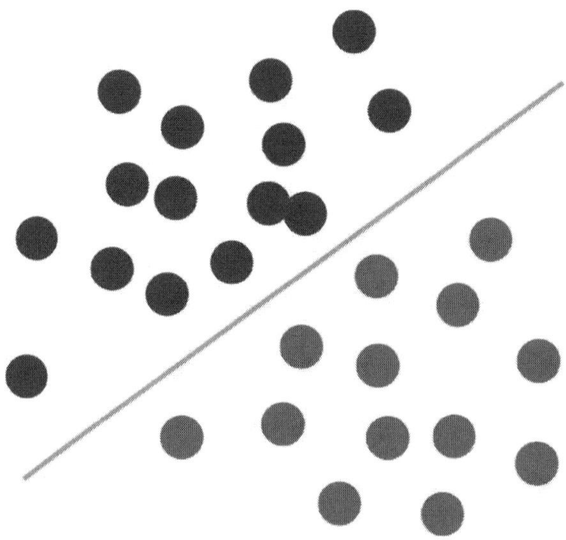

But in many cases, this linear approach totally fails. For instance, like in this example, we can't separate the blue and red circulars by drawing a straight line between them:

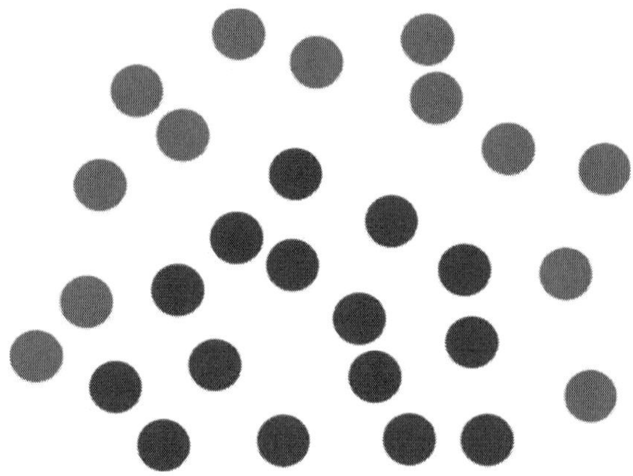

Anyway, linear separation in multidimensional spaces is not that trivial. Because of this, perceptrons are still used for some practical tasks.

However, the limitations of perceptron learning capabilities are profound. For example, perceptrons can't even learn the XOR logic function. By the way, this limitation caused one of the major setbacks in the history of artificial neural networks in the 1970s.

The logic functions can be regarded as atomic building blocks for any computations. Even tremendously sophisticated computations can be reduced to applying the basic logic functions: AND, OR, and NOT.

The XOR function gives the following mapping:

(0, 0) → 0, (0, 1) → 1, (1, 0) → 1, (1, 1) → 0.

Therefore, a perceptron cannot separate the group {(0, 1), (1,0)} and the group {(0, 0), (1,1)}:

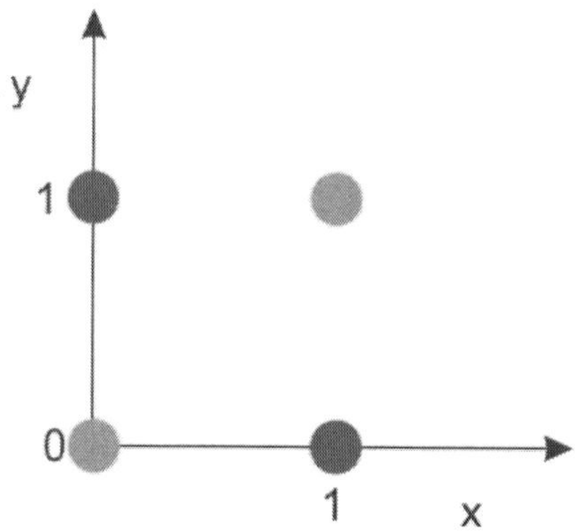

Although a single perceptron cannot implement the XOR function, it can implement the basic logic functions.

The XOR function can be obtained as a combination of several NOT and AND functions. This means if we combine several perceptrons together in one network, this aggregate structure will be able to learn the XOR function.

It can be done in the following way:

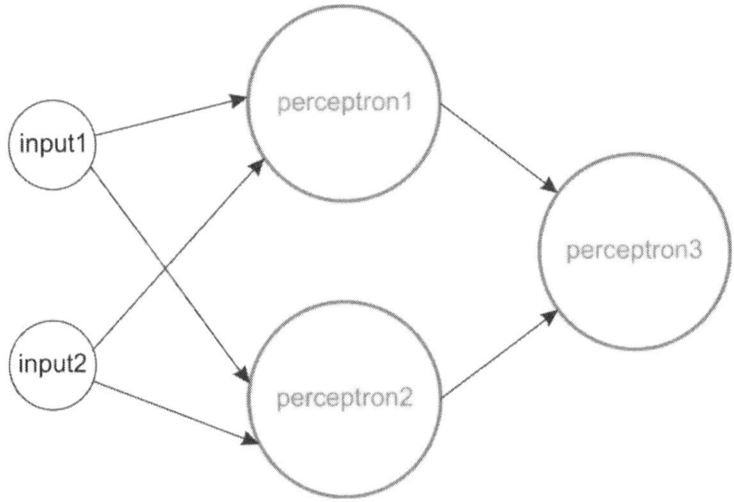

This structure is a neural network with one hidden layer, in which individual perceptrons can be viewed as neurons or nodes. Such structures are also called a multi-layer perceptron.

But for a long time, there was no efficient method for adjusting the values of weights in such aggregates of perceptrons. So, multi-layer perceptrons couldn't be used for solving tasks.

Only in the 1980s, a practical method for training multi-layer perceptrons had finally appeared. Actually, it was a reinvention of an older method that had been proposed for solving some other tasks. After that, neural networks started to slowly gain their popularity.

This miraculous method for training deep neural networks is called the *back-propagation algorithm* or just *backprop*. In essence, back-propagation is basically the chain rule from calculus, which I introduced in the previous chapter.

I should also mention that according to the so-called *universal approximation theorem*, a multi-layer perceptron with only one hidden layer is capable of approximating any function. But the hidden layer must grow exponentially with the size of the input. As a result, if we have a large number of input units – for example when working with pictures containing a large number of pixels – a network with one hidden layer becomes impractical.

Primarily because of this limitation, data scientists use neural networks with more than one hidden layers for solving complex tasks like, for example, image recognition. And such neural networks are considered deep. So, a deep neural network is a network with more than one hidden layer.

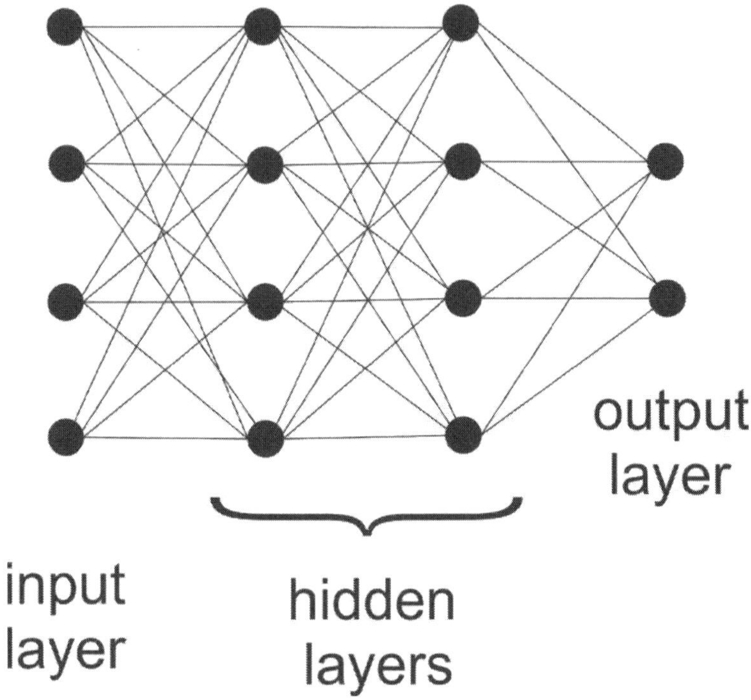

However, the term *deep neural network* is controversial. In recent publications, neural networks are called “deep” usually only if they have at least dozens of hidden layers.

So, let’s finally discuss in more detail how a typical deep neural network works.

An atomic component of a neural network is a neuron or node. As we just saw, a neuron in a neural network basically does what a perceptron does, but the weight adjustment is implemented in a different way.

A deep neural network usually consists of several layers of neurons.

Some state-of-the-art deep neural networks have hundreds of hidden layers.

The neurons in an input layer do not make any computations and just hold the values which are processed in the next layer.

In each neuron of the first hidden layer, the numbers coming from the input layer are multiplied by the weights and summed up together. The bias component is also usually added to this sum to make the network more flexible during training.

Then, this sum goes through a non-linear function. By the way, this nonlinearity is extremely important. If we didn't apply non-linear functions in neurons, we wouldn't get any advantage of using hidden layers at all, so in this situation we wouldn't really do deep learning. This non-linear function is called an *activation function*.

In addition to imposing non-linearity, some activation functions allow keeping the output of a neuron in a certain range of values, which is also important.

In theory, there are many activation functions which can be used, but only a few of them are used in practice. Shortly we'll return to activation functions and discuss them in detail.

The final result of a neuron is a single number. So, an entire layer of neurons produces a vector of a dimension which is equal to the number of the neurons in this layer. This vector is fed into the following layer of neurons, and this process continues up to the output layer.

Please note that the weights in one layer of neurons can be represented as a matrix. So, the whole process which constitutes the propagation of the input to the output in a neural net can be viewed as a series of vector-matrix multiplications. In Python, it can be built by using Numpy arrays. But these days we can build deep neural networks in a much simpler way, using modern frameworks for deep learning. And later in this book I'll show how to do that. Though knowing how to work with Numpy is still a mandatory skill if you want to do data analysis in Python.

Let's get back to our discussion of how neural networks work. So, after obtaining the fist output, our network cannot do anything useful - unless we're supernaturally lucky – because the network has to adjust its weights and biases, which are also called parameters or free parameters. The process of learning in a neural network is nothing more than adjusting its free parameters.

There are many ways how neural networks can do learning, which can be divided into three major general categories.

The first category represents the *Hebbian learning*, named after psychologist Donald Hebb. This type of learning is very simple and can potentially produce amazing results in unsupervised machine learning, combing with genetic algorithms. In this case, a genetic algorithm tries to minimize some objective function, which in this case is called a fitness function. But this book is not about it.

The second category includes so-called *competitive learning*. Actually, this type of learning can be viewed as a subfield of the Hebbian learning. Competitive learning is used in self-organizing maps, for example, which represent special shallow neural networks for unsupervised learning. In this type of learning, the signal propagates just to one neuron or a small fraction of neurons. But this book is not about competitive learning either. By the way, if you're interested in neural networks which do competitive learning, you can check out my short e-book "Machine Learning with Clustering".

This book is all about *error-correction learning* in deep neural networks, which is our third category. In this type of learning, a neural network compares its actual output with its desired output. Unlike in competitive learning, the signals propagate throughout all the neurons in a neural network. It can be implemented in supervised and unsupervised ways. Reinforcement learning can also be done using error-correction learning in deep neural networks.

In a supervised way of learning, a neural network is given a training set that consists of data samples with labels. This data points usually reside in a highly-dimensional space. For example, it can contain pixel values if we're dealing with image-processing tasks such as image classification. For black and white images, each pixel value represents one dimension. Each label represents a class, for example, a dog or cat.

If we have, say, two classes, the output vector of a neural network for classification contains only two neurons. Each component represents a probability for belonging to one of the classes. A probability is a value in a range between 0 and 1.

When we use a network for classification, we want the component for the correct class to be close to 1 and other components close to 0. Classification problems are also called logistic regression problems.

In a supervised way of learning, we can also build a network for regression problems. Regression is the process of finding the values for a dependant variable given the values of independent variables. Regression can be either linear or non-linear. Regression can also be single variable or multi-variable. Single variable regression can be depicted on a 2-dimensional plot. Of course, there is no practical need to use deep neural networks for single variable regression problems.

If we build a neural network for regression problems, the output layer should contain only one neuron because this network produces a vector with one component whose value corresponds to the value of the dependant variable.

Regression problems are very common in data analysis. For example, when we want to predict the price for a house given its parameters like its square area and other characteristics, we have a typical regression problem. However, deep neural networks are more frequently used for solving classification problems than for regression.

In either case of regression or classification, during training, a neural network compares its actual output with the desired output, or in other words with its label value. In this process, a neural network computes an objective function or loss function. There are many loss functions, which we'll discuss in more detail later. *The process of training a neural network is nothing more than minimizing the loss function by the adjustment of the weights and biases.* This adjustment is implemented through a process called gradient descent.

As you may recall from the preceding chapter, a gradient is a vector of partial derivatives. A partial derivative shows how a function changes at a specific point with respect to one dimension. In particular, a partial derivative shows whether a function increases or decreases.

Gradient descent can be explained by the following equation:

$$w_{i(new)} = w_{i(old)} - \eta \frac{\partial E}{\partial w_{i(old)}},$$

where

η – the learning rate

$\frac{\partial E}{\partial w_{i(old)}}$ *– gradient of the loss function with respect to a parameter* w_i

$w_{i(new)}$ *– new value of a parameter* w_i

$w_{i(old)}$ *– previous value of a parameter* w_i

In this process, a new value for a parameter is found by subtracting a partial derivative with respect to this parameter multiplied by the special number called a *learning rate* from the previous value. The learning rate is one of the hyper-parameters of a neural network. It is not surprising that choosing an appropriate value for a learning rate is important. It's a good idea to keep a learning rate smaller. But if a learning rate is too small, it can significantly slow down the training.

The gradient-based optimization boils down to the iterative process of finding global minima of functions. Gradient descent can get stuck in one of the local minima of a function instead of finding its global minima. This problem is known as the *local minima problem*. For a long time in the machine learning community, this problem had been considered to be one of the major drawbacks of using neural networks. But it turns out that neural networks which have many learnable parameters are almost completely insusceptible to this problem. In such networks, the gradient descent algorithm indeed almost always gets stuck in local minima, but those local minima are almost as good as the global minimum itself, so this is not really a big problem. In general, the larger the number of learnable parameters in a neural network, the less susceptible this networks becomes to the local minima problem.

In a deep neural network, partial derivatives with respect to the network's free parameters (weights and biases) are computed by using the back-propagation algorithm.

Each hidden layer in a neural network can be viewed as a function whose input is the output of the preceding layer. If you understand this, it's great.

For example, a neural network with three hidden layers f_3, f_2, and f_1 can be viewed as the composite function $E(f_3(f_2(f_1(x))))$, where E is a loss function. Then if we want to find the derivative of E with respect to f_1, we can use the chain rule:

$$\frac{dE}{df_1} = \frac{dE}{df_3}\frac{df_3}{df_2}\frac{df_2}{df_1}$$

But in order to be able to train a neural network, we need to find how ***E*** changes with respect not only to the layers but to all the individual free parameters of the network, so we should use partial derivatives.

In neural networks with back-propagation, there is the so-called *vanishing gradient problem*. Back-propagation is basically just the chain rule, and the chain rule is just multiplication of derivatives. The thing is if we multiply numbers whose absolute values are smaller than 1, their product will be even smaller than any of these numbers, and with each additional multiplication, the product gets smaller and smaller. From the gradient descent equation, we can see that vanishingly small gradients prevent a neural network's parameters from changing their values. In general, the greater the number of layers in a neural network, the more susceptible this network can get to the vanishing gradient problem. In some situations because of this problem, parameters in earlier layers of a neural network may completely stop being updated.

On the contrary, when we multiply many numbers whose absolute values are greater than 1, the absolute number of the product can be very large. This situation is just a flip side of the vanishing gradient problem known as exploding gradients, and it can also be very bad for training neural networks.

The vanishing/exploding gradient problem is one of the biggest and central problems in deep learning, if not the biggest problem. Feed-forward neural networks with many layers and recurrent neural networks – which we'll discuss later – are highly susceptible to this problem.

The vanishing gradient problem was first identified back in 1991. Since then, a significant portion of algorithm improvements in deep learning has been designed specifically to overcome or at least diminish this problem. For example, such improvements include superior neural network architectures (LSTM, residual networks), better activation functions, smarter methods for weight initialization, and advanced optimization algorithms.

I should say that when we code deep neural networks, our frameworks for deep learning implement back-propagation for us automatically, and what we only need is to specify the pass for forward propagation or even only the structure of our networks. Because of this, we don't really need to understand how back-propagation works in details to build deep learning models in practice. If you don't really like math but want to start building neural networks as soon as possible, I recommend you not spend much time on how back-propagation works. But anyway, at least a basic understanding of backprop is super helpful for working with neural networks.

The training process of a typical deep neural network includes the following stages:

1 Forward propagation

2 Computing the loss function

3 Back-propagation (computing the gradients)

4 One step of gradient descent

5 Stop if we have reached the minimum or used the specified number of iterations.

6 Go to the first stage

The stage of gradient descent can be implemented in several different ways. The thing is, we can use all or only some training examples for one step of gradient descent. If we use all the training examples, we implement so-called *full-batch gradient descent*. In this case, for each training example we compute a cost function. So, a cost function is an error function for a single training example. After forward-propagation of all training examples, we compute a loss function and implement one step of gradient descent. In this case, the loss function is just an average of all the cost functions. Full-batch gradient descent is a computationally expensive strategy (due to its huge memory requirements), woefully slow on large datasets and not usually applied for training deep neural networks in practice. Another disadvantage of full-batch gradient descent is that it doesn't allow for online learning. It means we need to have all the training data before implementing the training process.

The other variation of gradient descent is *mini-batch gradient descent*. In this case, a training set is randomly divided into a certain number of mini-batches. For example, if the training set includes 100.000 examples, and the size for a mini-batch (batch size) equals 100, then we have 100.000/100 = 1000 mini-batches. One step of gradient descent is implemented for each mini-batch during the training cycle. The size of an efficient mini-batch crucially depends on the characteristics of the hardware. As a general rule, the more computationally powerful hardware, the larger size for a mini-batch can be set. It is recommended to keep the value of a batch size as a number of power 2, for example, 64, 128, 256, 512, 1024.

Here, I also should mention that one iteration through an entire training set is called an *epoch*. Therefore, full-batch gradient descent implements one step for an epoch; whereas, mini-batch gradient descent implements many steps for a single epoch.

The third major type of gradient descent is called *stochastic gradient descent* or *SGD*. In this case, one step of gradient descent is implemented for *each* training example, which is chosen randomly in each iteration of the training. In SGD, the cost and lost functions coincide with each other. For one epoch, in the case of SGD, the number of gradient descent steps is equal to the number of training examples.

But please note that the terms "SGD" and "stochastic gradient descent" are also frequently applied when mini-batch gradient descent is used, and we can encounter this usage of these terms in research papers very often. By the way, it used to be incredibly confusing to me.

It turns out that introducing some additional parameters and adjustments can significantly improve the vanilla gradient descent algorithms. One of such parameters is a *learning rate decay*. If a learning rate is constant, it either slows down the training at the initial stages (small learning rate) or prevents gradient descent from convergence (large learning rate).

Instead, what we often need is to keep a learning rate relatively large at the beginning of training and relatively small at the end, so we use a learning rate decay. This parameter allows taking smaller steps of gradient descent as the training progresses.

Another important parameter which can improve gradient descent is *momentum*. This parameter dampens oscillations of gradient descent and allows using a larger learning rate, so it accelerates the training.

Some sophisticated implementations of gradient descent like the so-called *RMSprop algorithm* allow adjusting learning rates for individual free parameters. It's also a great addition to vanilla gradient descent.

Another sophisticated algorithm combines RMSprop with momentum. This algorithm is called *Adam*.

State-of-the-art frameworks for deep learning allow us to treat different gradient descent algorithms as black boxes and don't worry too much about the math behind these algorithms. Deep learning is much easier now than it was a few years ago. But anyway we need to know how to adjust optimal parameters of those algorithms. As a general rule, we can use the default parameters of the algorithms in most cases. In the final chapters of this book, we'll be working with the Keras

API for deep learning. Keras provides seven different algorithms for gradient descent, including RMSprop and Adam. You can check them out at https://keras.io/optimizers/.

All the algorithms we just discussed belong to gradient-based optimization. In addition to gradient-based optimization, there are some alternative methods of optimization which can be in principle used in deep neural networks. However, gradient descent with back-propagation has proved to be the most efficient way among all the methods of optimization for training deep neural networks even though it has its own disadvantages like the vanishing/exploding gradient problem.

Now let me say a few more things about functions in the context of deep learning. We've already encountered a couple of different functions in our discussion of deep networks. Please don't confuse an activation function with an objective function. An activation function is implemented for each neuron in a network (except for the input neurons and for the output layer neuron in regression tasks). Whereas, a single objective function is implemented for an entire neural network.

Also, try to think about a neural network as a function itself, which has many independent variables, the number of which equals the number of the input neurons. Regardless of the task a neural network is built for – such as image recognition, speech recognition, regression, natural language process and others – the network always maps the input to the output. Our goal is to get the network to map appropriate outputs for its inputs, by adjusting the parameters of the network.

There is always a function for any process in the universe. Let's call this function *U*. It can be a quite simple function, but for more complex processes this function gets more complicated. A neural network as a function has to approximate the *U* function by adjusting the parameters of its own function in a right way. Apparently, if the network has more parameters, it can better approximate the *U* function. Moreover, as some recent papers demonstrate, applying additional layers to the network can exponentially reduce the overall number of required parameters.

So, a deep neural network tries to approximate some *U* function by minimizing its objective function during training in order to find an appropriate set of its free parameters for its own function. In this whole process, there are three distinct main functions we should care for:

1 *U* function

2 The network itself as a compound function

3 Objective function

I think having this intuition behind neural networks can be helpful.

There are two main phases in the work of a neural network: training and inference. Usually, the training stage is much more computationally expensive than the inference stage.

Having trained a network, then we should validate the network's performance on new data before using it in production (the inference stage). So, in addition to a training set, we should have one more data set – a validation set. It may be possible that our network works perfectly on a training set but poorly on a validation set. Most likely it happens because of the process called *overfitting*.

Overfitting occurs when a machine learning algorithm like a neural network just remembers its training examples by heart, so to speak, but cannot generalize on new data. There are a number of techniques for avoiding overfitting in deep neural networks, which we'll discuss later.

After successful validation, we should test a neural network on new data. So, we should have one more dataset for doing this – a test dataset. If a network works great on a test set, it can be finally used in production.

Activation functions

Now let's take a closer look at different activation functions which we can use in deep neural networks.

As we've seen, the input of an activation function is the weighted sum of a neuron's inputs plus a bias. And as I've already mentioned, an activation function has to be non-linear. In most cases, all neurons in a single layer utilize only one type of activation function, but a neural network can have different activation functions in different layers.

First of all, there is a whole family of so-called *sigmoid activation functions*. These functions are called sigmoid because they have an s-like shape.

Probably, the most famous sigmoid function is the *logistic function*. The output of this function is a number between 0 and 1.

$$f(x) = \frac{1}{1 + e^{-x}}$$

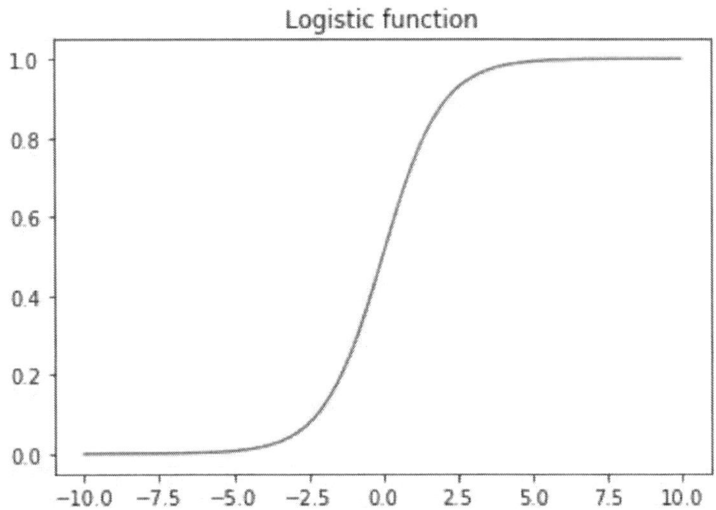

This function was very widely used in deep neural networks in the past. But today it is mostly used only in an output layer in networks for binary logistic regression.

The major problem with this function is that its derivatives in most places are unacceptably close to 0. Therefore, neural networks with this activation functions in their hidden layers are highly susceptible to the vanishing gradient problem.

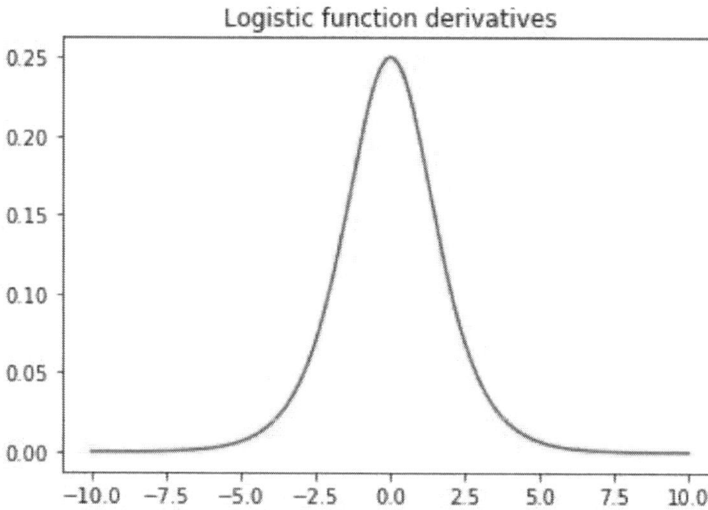

The other problem with the logistic function is that this function gives 0.5 when the input is 0. But when the input is zero, we want the output to be close to zero. For this reason, some other sigmoid activation functions that do not share this characteristic are more often used in neural networks.

For example, one of such sigmoid functions is the *hyperbolic tangent*.

$$f(x) = \frac{e^x - e^{-x}}{e^x - e^{-x}}$$

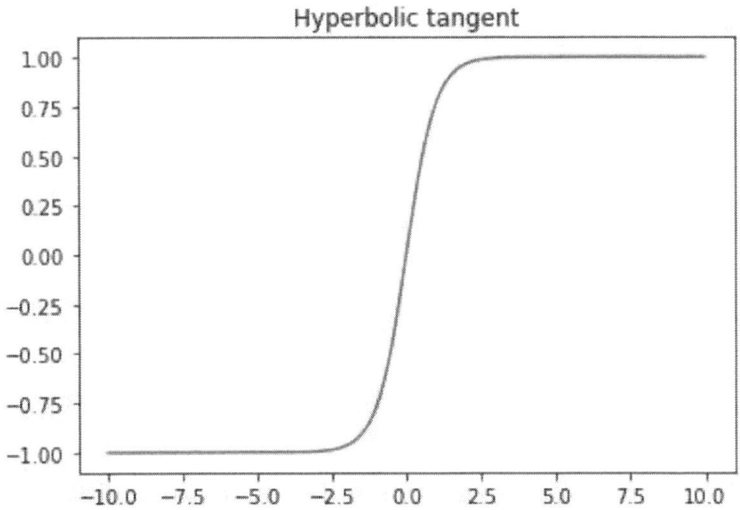

This function also suffers from the fact that its derivatives are often very close to zero.

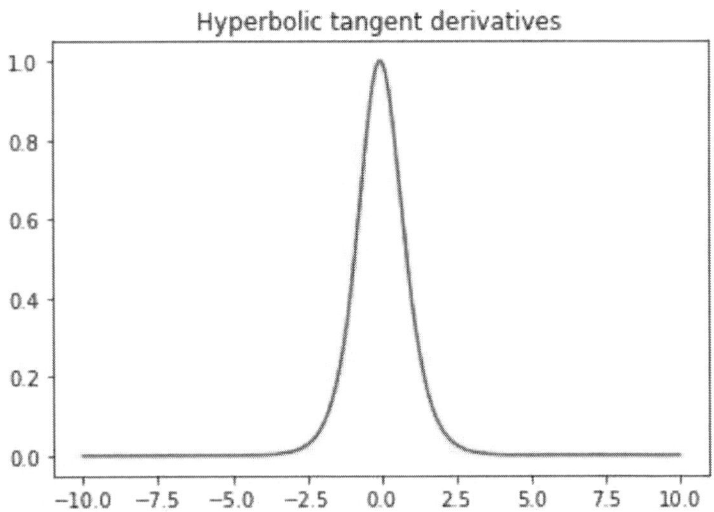

This function is used in some special cases we'll talk about in this book later.

One realization of the logistic function for multiclass logistic regression is the *softmax function*. Softmax calculates the probabilities of each class over all possible classes. The output of this function is a number between 0 and 1, and the sum of all the outputs is equal to 1. As the logistic function, Softmax is used as an activation function in the final layer. In this case, the number of neurons in the final layer is equal to the number of classes, and each neuron represents a probability of belonging to one class.

$$f(x) = \frac{e^{z_l}}{\sum e^{z_l}}$$

This formula computes the exponential of the given neuron value and the sum of exponential values of all the values of the neurons in the last layer. Then the ratio of the exponential of the given neuron value and the sum of exponential values of all the neurons in the last layer is the output of this function.

For example, let's say we have three classes; therefore we have three neurons in the final layer. Before applying the activation function, we have the following linear components of the values of the neurons in the final layer: [4, 2, -1]

So, the e^z values from our formula are

$e^4 = 54,7$

$e^2 = 7,4$

$e^{-1} = 0,4$

The sum of these values is

54,7 + 7,4 + 0,4 = 62,5

Now we can compute the probabilities for each class:

softmax1 = 54,7/62,5 =0,8752

softmax2 = 7,4/62,5 =0,1184

softmax3 = 0,4/62,5 =0,0064

Currently, the most commonly used activation function for deep neural networks is the *rectified linear unit (ReLU)*. It's very simple: for all its negative inputs it gives 0, and for all its positive ones, the output equals the input.

$$f(x) = \max(0, x)$$

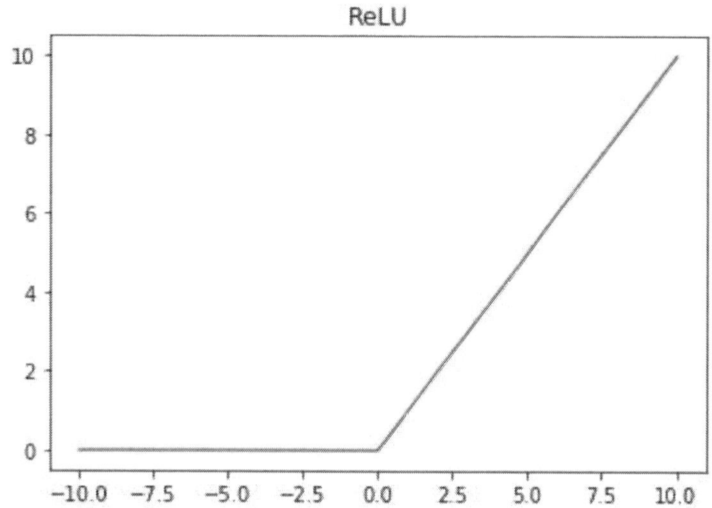

The derivative of this function for all positive outputs is simply 1, and it is very convenient. So, this activation function is easy to compute, and its derivatives are also easy to compute.

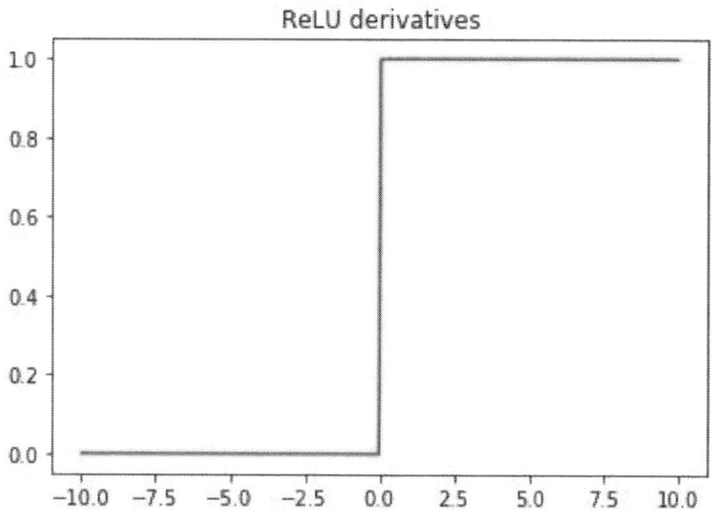

The ReLU is not differentiable at zero, but it's not really a problem for modern frameworks for deep learning. This function has some other problem which is more important. As the ReLU converts the outputs of neurons to zero approximately 50% of the time, it can prevent a significant amount of neurons in the network from updating its parameters during training.

To confront this problem and preserve the advantages of ReLU, there is another activation function – so-called LeakyReLU. It's almost ReLU, but for negative inputs, its output is not zero.

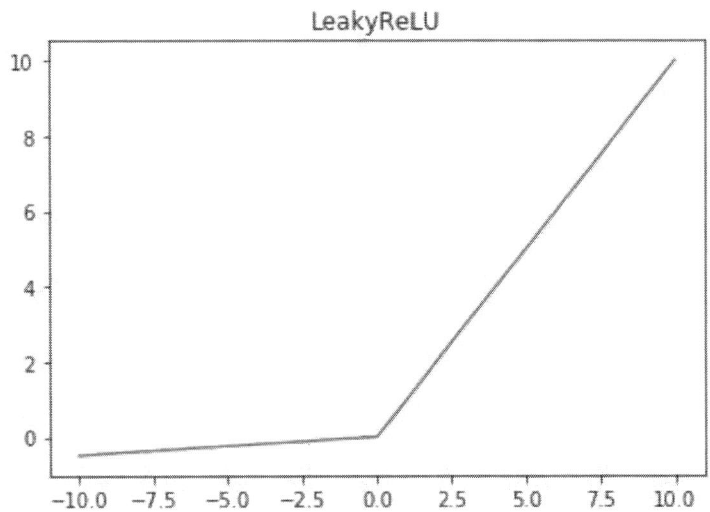

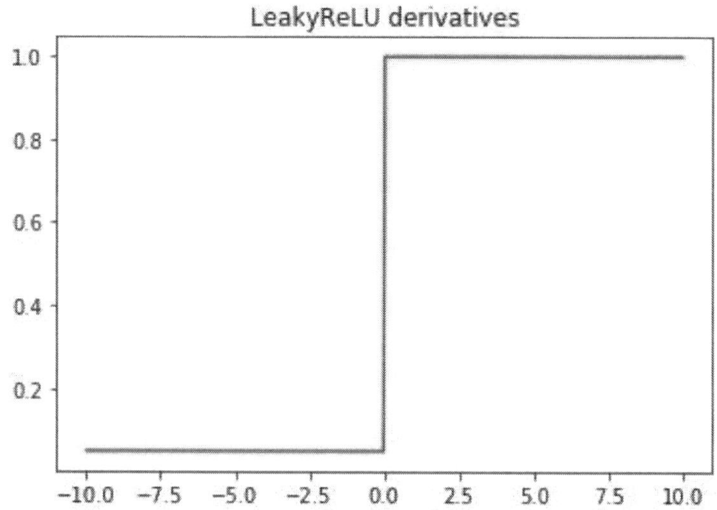

There is also another activation function with similar properties: the exponential linear unit (ELU):

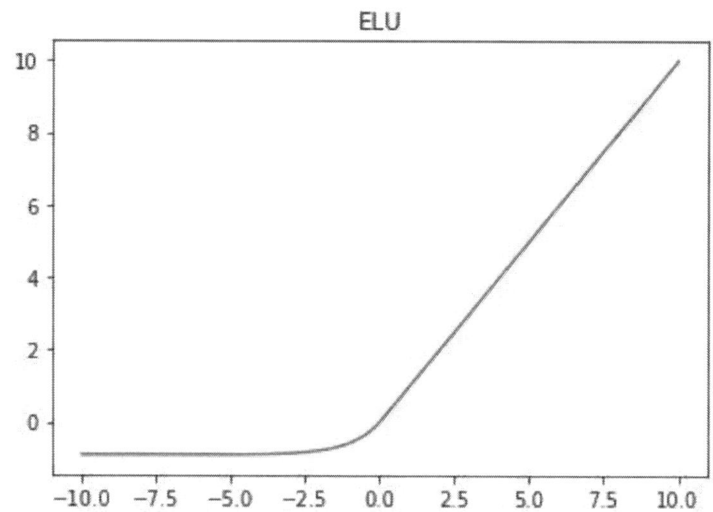

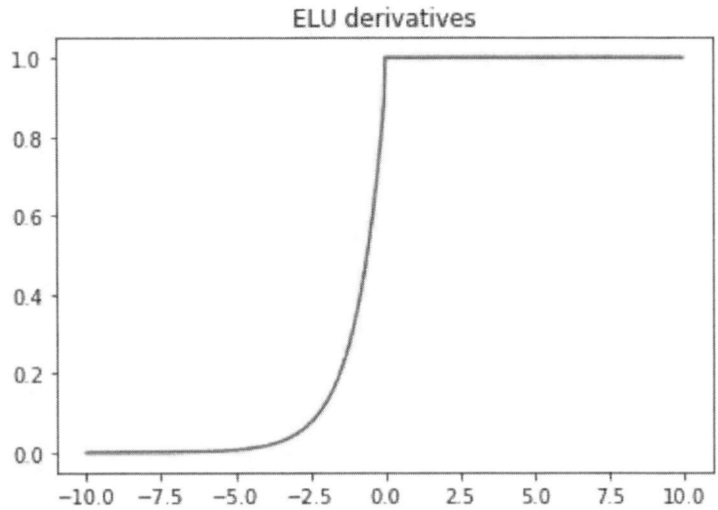

In addition to all of these functions, there are many other activation functions, but they are extremely rarely used in practice.

Loss and cost functions

The key principle of error-correction learning is the minimization of the difference between actual and ideal output. And this is the essence of machine learning in general.

Loss and cost functions are often treated as synonymous in machine learning jargon. They are also sometimes called objective and error functions. In the context of deep neural networks, a cost function is usually referred to the function that computes the error for one training sample; whereas, a loss function is the average of cost functions. A loss function also often includes some additional terms for regularization, which I'll explain shortly.

There are many loss functions for neural networks. For example, Keras API provides 14 different loss functions. Several widely-used loss functions in deep neural networks include Binary Cross Entropy, Categorical Cross Entropy, and Mean Squared Error.

For example, the squared error loss function is extremely simple and intuitive. It's just the average squared difference between the predicted and expected values:

$$MSE = \frac{1}{N}\sum_{i=0}^{N}\left(y_i - \hat{y}_i\right)^2,$$

Where

N – number of samples

y_i *– predicted value*

$\hat{y}_i$ *– expected value*

Cross-entropy loss functions are probably a little bit trickier and less intuitive than the Mean Squared Error function. First of all, I should say that *Cross-entropy* is a category from Information Theory for measuring the distance between probability distributions. In turn, *entropy* is the term from physics for measuring order/disorder. In neural networks for classification, cross-entropy measures the distance between the probability distribution which is produced by a neural network for classification and the distribution of the true values or labels.

Choosing the right loss function is extremely important because different loss functions are best suited for different types of tasks. For example, the cross-entropy family of loss functions usually works very well in neural networks with sigmoid activation functions in the last layer, so these functions are used for classification tasks which output probabilities. Whereas, using the Mean Squared Error is a standard for doing regression tasks. Connectionist temporal classification (CTC) is a loss function which is used for some sequence learning tasks. Some other tasks require using more special and even exotic loss functions. And sometimes, new tasks even require building unique loss functions for them.

Weight initialization and batch normalization

In theory, regardless in which way we initialize the weights, a neural network can be able to learn. But in practice, deep neural networks are very sensitive to weight initialization. The method of initializing parameters affects the training process greatly. In particular, a proper choice of weight initialization can reduce the vanishing/exploding gradient problem. So, we should initialize the weights for our neural networks properly.

Usually, the initializing of the weights of a neural network as the normal distribution with a mean of 0 and a variance of 1 works quite well. For example, it works better than initializing all weights as zeroes or ones.

However, it has been shown that the standard deviation of the normal distribution for weight initialization should be less than 1. It was estimated that the standard deviation should be **1/√n** or **2/√n**, where **n** is the number of weights connected to a given neuron from the previous layer.

The choice of a proper weight initialization in a given layer depends on what activation function is used in the previous layer of the network. The standard deviation of **1/√n** for weight initialization works best for sigmoid activation functions. But for the ReLU activation function, the standard deviation of **2/√n** is more preferable.

There is the so-called *xavier initialization* that exploits the standard deviations of **1/√n** and **2/√n**. Currently, the xavier initialization is the most common type of weight initialization for deep neural networks.

There are two main variations of this initialization: normal and uniform. In the Keras API, the uniform xavier initialization is used as a default method of weight initialization.

Bias initialization is also important, but it is simpler than the proper weight initialization. In principle, we don't necessarily need to have biases at all. But adding biases to the neurons gives additional flexibility of the model. It's common practice to initialize biases as zeros.

It turns out that not only do we need to initialize the parameters in the right way, but we also often need to keep the parameters in certain ranges of values during the training process. We can do it by using a very powerful technique in deep learning called *batch normalization*.

As I’ve already mentioned, working with normalized data is always better. But in addition to just normalizing the input data, we can also normalize the outputs of the hidden layers during training at each batch, hence the name batch normalization.

Batch normalization can be implemented in two different ways: we can either normalize learnable parameters (weights and biases) or the outputs of activation functions.

When we use batch normalization, we can use higher learning rates, which can significantly speed up training. Also, batch normalization allows for deeper networks by reducing the vanishing gradient problem and adding some other effects. Some popular deep neural networks do not properly work at all without using batch normalization.

Overfitting and underfitting and methods to overcome them in deep neural networks

The problem of overfitting/underfitting is certainly one of the central topics in all machine learning, including deep neural networks. In data science jargon, it common to say that underfitting models have high bias and models that overfit have high variance.

When we deal with underfitting, it implies that our model is too general, or in other words over-simplistic. Conversely, overfitting occurs when our model is too specific that describes nearly perfect training data but cannot generalize well on new data.

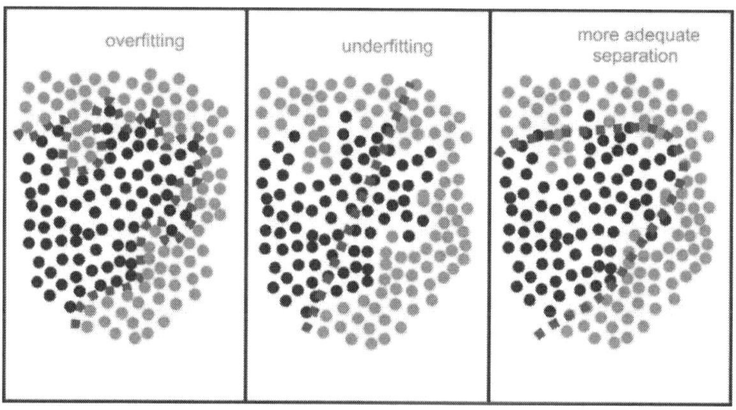

Overfitting can be viewed as the memorization of training data by a machine learning model. Overfitting is an especially common problem in deep learning due to the complexity of deep neural networks.

Our goal is avoiding occurring both overfitting and underfitting. In traditional machine learning algorithms, there is usually some quite noticeable tradeoff between underfitting and overfitting. In this case, we cannot reduce overfitting greatly without ending up with a situation where we start underfitting the data and vice versa. The good news is that in deep neural networks this tradeoff is less dramatic.

In order to reduce underfitting in deep neural networks, we should build more complex models by adding more hidden layers and neurons. Adding additional hidden layers is more preferable strategy than adding just neurons to avoid underfitting, but, of course, we should also remember about the vanishing gradient problem. Also, we can train the neural network longer by increasing the number of epochs.

The main strategies for avoiding overfitting in deep neural networks include:

Early stopping

Adding more training data

Augmentation of existing data

Regularization

Batch normalization

Dropout

By reducing the number of epochs, we can reduce overfitting. There are certain practical techniques – some of which we'll discuss later –provided by modern deep learning frameworks which can help determine the optimal number of epochs during training. We can measure the accuracy of our model after each epoch. As a general rule, we should stop training when the performance of the model is no longer increasing on validation data. This approach is quite efficient in reducing overfitting and probably should be used in every neural network that has a tendency to overfit its training data. However, using only this strategy does not always guarantee sufficient overfitting prevention. Moreover, using this technique alone can hamper neural network performance.

Adding more training data is maybe the best method to reduce ovefitting, but oftentimes this strategy is the hardest one, especially for practical real-world problems. It can be even the case that data for training a given deep model do not exist at all and we need somehow to make them. Moreover, for supervised machine learning tasks, we need to provide each sample with a corresponding label. It may sound counterintuitive, but in order to automate some task with the help of deep learning, first we may need much labor to do this very task by humans. Also, having significantly more training data leads to the need for more computational resources.

If we have some amount of data for our deep neural network, sometimes we can make new data from the existing data. This strategy is called data augmentation. For example, if we work with image recognition, we can produce new images by rotating existing images in our training dataset. It is extremely helpful that some frameworks for deep learning enable us to do this task automatically with a line of code. And we can do other manipulations with images like adding random noise, stretching, or squeezing. Data augmentation methods with images are depended on the task we're working on. For some tasks we cannot apply some methods. Data augmentation can also be used for working with sound.

Another strategy is called regularization. Regularization is probably a more sophisticated technique for overfitting reduction. But again it can be easily implemented in modern frameworks for deep learning and as such it's a very reliable method. As I mentioned in one of the previous chapters, regularization implies adding external terms to the objective function. In short, regularization penalizes large weights.

There are two main types of regularization: L1 and L2:

L1 regularization

$$E_{improved} = E_{original} + \alpha \sum_{i} w_i$$

L2 regularization

$$E_{improved} = E_{original} + \alpha \sum_{i} w_i^2$$

Where

E – loss function

α – *regularization parameter*

w_i – *weights*

In these formulas, *regularization parameter* is one of hyper-parameters of neural networks whose appropriate value we should find, usually by trial and error.

The intuition behind why regularization prevents overfitting is that a deep neural network does not use any feature too much in making predictions when we use regularization because all the weights during gradient descent hold more uniformly-spread values.

In most cases, L2 regularization works much better. But in some situations, L1 regularization excels. L1 is beneficial when our training data is very noisy. In particular, this is often the case in robotics. Moreover, in L1 regularization, some weights can be reduced to zeros, which can improve computational complexity of the model. But when we don't need to decrease computational complexity of the model and our data is not extremely noisy, L2 is a much more preferable strategy.

Batch normalization, which I introduced in the previous section, has also slight regularization effect. So, it prevents overfitting to some extent. But it is recommended to use batch normalization together with other methods for overfitting reduction in neural networks such as dropout.

Dropout is another good technique to reduce overfitting, maybe even more powerful than regularization. Dropout refers to random removing neurons in a neural network for each epoch during the training process. But after the network is trained, the complete network with all its neurons is used in the inference stage. Obviously, when we apply dropout, the neural network losses some number of its learnable parameters. Therefore, this technique makes deep models simpler during training and less susceptible to overfitting. But there is one more reason why dropout reduces overfitting. Since we apply dropout randomly for each epoch, the neurons do not tend to rely heavily on individual weights. Similarly to applying regularization, a deep neural network with dropout does not use any feature too much to make predictions.

We can implement dropout in some individual or all hidden layers of the network. The dropout ratio is the parameter that specifies the fraction of neurons being knocked out.

Finally, in order to reduce overfitting we often need to keep our deep models simpler meaning with fewer hidden layers. Moreover, for many tasks, we don't necessarily need to use deep learning at all and can use simpler machine learning algorithms.

Training, Validating and Testing

As I mentioned in the chapter on overview of deep learning, after training we should always validate and test our models. Also, we often need to tune our deep models by changing their hyper-parameters and repeat the cycle of training-validating-testing many times until the performance of our model is good enough. In order to do so, we need to randomly split our data into three separate datasets: a training set, a validation set (also called development set), and a testing set. Ideally, all the three sets should belong to the same distribution of data. But it's especially important that the training and validation sets have originated from the same distribution. However, there is an exception to this rule if we apply transfer learning. It's also important that the data which the model will use in production should also belong to this distribution or at least be very similar to that.

For supervised tasks, training and validation sets have to be labeled, but a testing set can be unlabeled. I should say that modern frameworks for deep learning enable us to split datasets into training and validation sets automatically, which is extremely helpful.

After completing each epoch on a train set, our model is validated on a validation set. As such, we can observe the performance of our model after each epoch. Our goal is to get such a performance that will be high both on training and validation sets. In order to do so, we often need to tune and retune a lot of hyper-parameters of our model. You may ask what performance is high. It depends on the task we are working on. Basically, by high or appropriate performance, I mean such a performance which is at least acceptable for our task. After we obtained a model with appropriate performance on train and validation sets, we finally test our model on a test set.

In traditional machine learning algorithms, it's often recommended to keep the ratio for these three datasets as 60/20/20, meaning 60% of the data should belong to a train set, 20% to a validation set, and 20% to a test set.

However, in deep learning we usually have much more data samples than in traditional machine learning algorithms. We can have millions of data samples in some tasks for deep learning. In these situations, we can use a much more fraction of the data for training. For example, we can use 98% of data on a train set, 1% on a validation set, and 1% on a test set.

Obviously, in order to measure the performance of our deep models we need to have some type of metric.

One metric for classification is accuracy:

$$Accuracy = \frac{Number\ of\ Correct\ Preditions}{Total\ Number\ of\ Predictions}$$

Probably, accuracy is the most common metric due to its simplicity. But this simplicity has its disadvantages. The major problem with accuracy is that, in some situations, accuracy can be seemingly very high, but the model might be completely meaningless. For example, we have a training set for a binary classification problem, where we have say 100.000 samples of class A and 50 sample of class B. If our model always predicts class A, then we have 99.5% accuracy. But in this situation, the model is not useful at all.

There are other metrics that do not have this big disadvantage of the accuracy metric. For such metrics, we build a so-called *confusion matrix*. Actually, modern libraries for machine learning can do this automatically.

For a binary classification problem, a confusion matrix represents a table consisting of two rows and two columns:

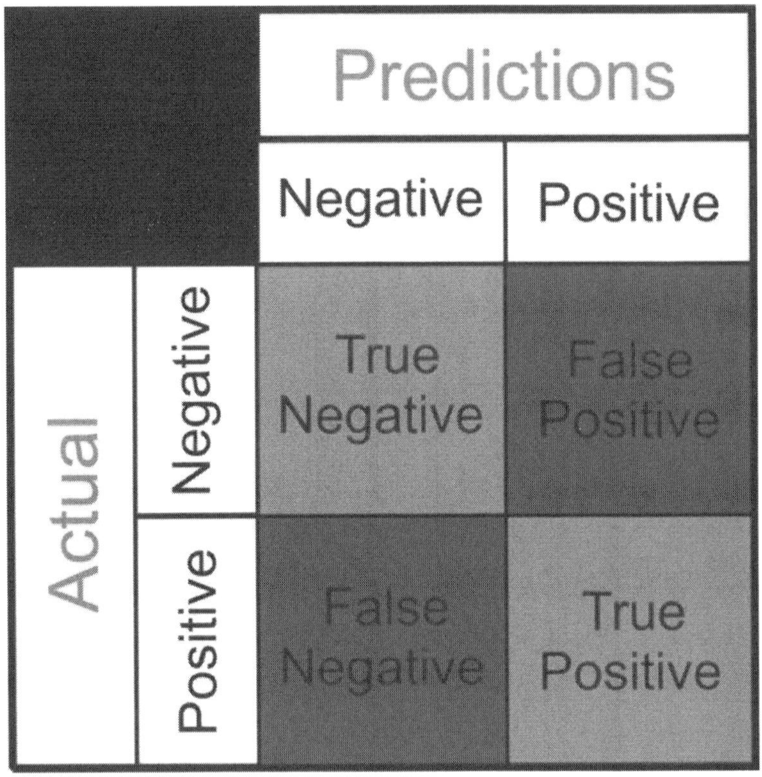

For multiclass classification, we can also build a confusion matrix. But this matrix would have more categories, depending on the number of classes.

As you can see, a confusion matrix for a binary classification problem splits all predictions into four categories: true positives, true negatives, false positives, and false negatives. Usually, the class with fewer samples (event) is considered positive.

true positive – correctly predicted event

true negative – correctly predicted no event

false positive – incorrectly predicted event

false negative – incorrectly predicted no event

For example, we can assign the presence of a certain disease as an event. If our model correctly predicted this presence for a specific sample, this prediction belongs to the true positive category. Conversely, if the model has failed to predict the presence of the disease, this prediction belongs to the false positive category. If the model correctly predicted no disease, this prediction belongs to the true negative category. And if the model incorrectly predicted no disease, this prediction belongs to the false negative category.

Based on these four categories, there are two general metrics: precision and recall.

$$Precision = \frac{True\ positives}{True\ positives + False\ positives}$$

$$Recall = \frac{True\ positives}{True\ positives + False\ negatives}$$

We should use either precision or recall, depending on the task we're working on. For instance, in our example with disease prediction, we should most likely penalize false positives; therefore, we should use the precision metric.

We can combine precision and recall into one metric. First, we can just take an average from precision and recall. But it's not the best strategy. A better approach to combine precision and recall is to take a harmonic mean from them. This metric is called *F1 score*:

$$F1\ Score = \frac{2 * Precision * Recall}{Precision + Recall}$$

The other problem with accuracy is that accuracy does not take into account uncertainty of predictions. When a neural network makes predictions on classification it always gives probabilities. For example, it can give a probability of 51% or 99% for a correct label in a binary classification task. Both those probabilities would be considered correct. And accuracy metric does not tell us anything about such uncertainties.

The other metric that confronts the problem of uncertainty in classification tasks is called *classification log loss*. This metric penalizes very confident wrong predictions and very unconfident correct perditions. This metric gives us a score. Our goal is to get that score as low as possible.

For evaluating regression tasks, we use other metrics. These metrics are very similar if not the same to loss functions for regression. One metric is Mean Square Error (MSE). The problem with this metric is that this metric doesn't give us numbers in the same set of units in our classification.

In order to avoid this limitation, we can simply take a square root from MSE. This is called the Root Mean Square Error (RMSE).

RMSE is more convenient and more commonly used metric than MSE. We can also use Mean Absolute Error (MAE). Our goal is to get RMSE, MSE, or MAE as low as possible, but not induce overfitting of course.

If the performance of our model is high on a training set but poor on a validation set, this is a sign of huge overfitting.

K-fold Cross validation is a very popular method for evaluating models in traditional machine learning algorithms. It can be used for evaluating both regression and classification. However, in deep learning, cross validation is not usually used because this method is much more demanded in computational resources. But it can be used if a deep model and especially a training set are quite small. Keras API for deep learning provides a scikit-learn interface enabling Keras models to be integrated into scikit-learn pipeline, where we can easily perform cross validation.

All the metrics we have just discussed are applicable only for supervised learning. Metrics for evaluating the performance of unsupervised learning problems are much trickier. Even more important, those metrics are often highly subjective. From my own experience, metrics for evaluating some unsupervised learning tasks are not used at all. In other situations, unsupervised learning tasks are manually evaluated by humans.

Transfer learning

In my opinion, transfer learning is one of the most amazing topics in deep learning. Transfer learning refers to the process where we take a model that has been trained for one task and use it for some other task. Of course, these tasks have to be similar to each other. The main idea behind transfer learning is that low-level representations which have been already learned by one model can be helpful for other models as well.

Transfer learning especially comes in handy given these three facts about training deep models: first, training deep neural networks requires significant computational resources, second, takes a lot of time, and, third, tends to be enormously greedy for training data. Transfer learning is particularly helpful when we have massive amounts of data for one task and a very limited amount of data for the other task.

On the web, there are many pre-trained for certain tasks deep models available for free that can be used for other tasks. For example, some such networks can be used in Tensorflow and Keras frameworks for deep learning, which is especially helpful. Keras provides ten pre-trained deep networks, which you can find here: https://keras.io/applications/. Two pre-trained networks provided by Keras have more than a hundred million parameters each, and one of the networks contains 572 layers. So, luckily for us, in many cases we don't need to construct and train our deep neural networks completely from scratch. It's especially the case for image processing tasks.

Let's move to the technical aspects of transfer learning. There are many schemes for implementing transfer learning. In one situation, we can take a neural network that has been trained on some data, remove its output layer, and change it to a new output layer. Then we can train this network on new data. Of course, in this situation, the dimension of our feature vectors has to remain the same as the dimension of the data this model has been pre-trained on.

We can also replace more than just the output layer alone. It largely depends on how similar the tasks are. If the tasks are not very similar, we can use only a few first layers from the pre-trained model.

We can either freeze the parameters imported from the pre-trained model or let back-propagation modify them if we have enough data. If we don't have much data and we unfreeze the parameters from the pre-trained model, we will very likely induce huge overfitting in our model.

If the inputs are not the same, we can replace the input layer. Also, we can use a preprocessing data step to resize the input to the needed size if possible.

As I said, transfer learning is mostly applicable for visual processing tasks, but it can be also applied for audio processing, Natural Language Processing (NLP), and other tasks.

In particular, it can be applied to reinforcement learning. A very interesting approach, which is employed in deep reinforcement learning, is so-called *progressive neural networks* (https://arxiv.org/abs/1606.04671). This approach has been developed by the researchers from DeepMind. Progressive neural networks can be used for reinforcement learning, for instance, in robotics. As the researchers say this approach is an important step to building artificial general intelligence because a progressive neural network can learn how to perform a whole series of different tasks. These networks can be used in supervised learning as well.

A progressive neural net represents a combination of several linked-up deep networks, which are called columns. In a progressive network, each column is trained for performing only one specific task. A column that is being trained can use some information from previously trained columns; moreover, the previously trained columns do not rewrite their weights in this process. However, there are certain drawbacks to this approach. The more columns in a progressive neural network, the harder this network learns new tasks. So, these networks are weakly scalable, at least now.

Even a more amazing approach to transfer learning has been proposed in this paper by researchers form Google Brain: https://arxiv.org/abs/1806.11146. They managed to force a neural network to perform new task that it had never done before by applying so-called *adversarial attacks*.

How to set up optimal hyper-parameters for deep models

So far, we have covered a lot of material on general principles and techniques of deep learning. Before jumping into specialized architectures of deep neural networks, we should briefly discuss how we choose optimal hyper-parameters for our deep models.

Recall, optimal learnable parameters (weights and biases in neural networks) are learned by a machine learning algorithm, but hyper-parameters at the first place should be specified by humans, at least until Skynet is not around.

Hyper-parameters for deep neural networks include:

The number of hidden layers

The number of neurons in the layers

Weight initialization

The learning rate

Activation functions

Loss function

The number of epochs

This list is not exhaustive. For example, if we use mini-batch gradient descent, we need to specify the size of a mini-batch, or if we use regularization, we need to specify the regularization parameter.

The choice of the optimal hyper-parameters depends on many various factors. One of such factors is a type of the hardware which we're going to use for training deep models. First of all, we should consider how much computer memory we have and whether we use a CPU, GPU, or TPU (more on that later).

And when we're building a deep neural network, we shouldn't reinvent the wheel. We should look for similar problems and find out how they've been solved before with deep neural networks. So, we can incorporate the values at least of some hyper-parameters from those networks if possible. Moreover, there are many pre-trained models available on the web which we often can use for developing our own networks.

In addition to all of that, I should say that setting optimal hyper-parameters for deep learning is a highly empirical process. By that, I mean that we often need to try many configurations of hyper-parameters to determine the right ones. In his course on deep learning, Andrew Ng proposes two main strategies for setting hyper-parameters. The first strategy implies a gradual iterative changing of hyper-parameters values for a single model. The other strategy suggests using many neural networks with different hyper-parameters in parallel or iteratively (it takes much more time) and choosing the best one in the end. These strategies can be and probably should be combined in one process: at first we try many neural networks with different hyper-parameters, choose the best network, and then tune different hyper-parameters of this network. If we're doing this manually, it's much better to tune only one hyper-parameter at a time.

Of course, training many deep neural networks in parallel is a very computationally expensive process and strictly limited by computational resources available to us.

Being able to tune deep neural networks effectively is one of the most important skills to master if one is serious about deep learning. Fortunately, modern frameworks for deep learning have some wonderful tools for tuning deep models. One of such tool is called TensorBoard, which we'll touch on later.

Also, choosing optimal values for hyper-parameters can be viewed as a machine learning or optimization problem itself. Genetic algorithms can be very helpful in solving this problem.

Genetic algorithms belong to a larger class of approaches called evolutionary algorithms, which in turn belong to non gradient-based optimization methods. By the way, genetic algorithms can be used as optimization methods in deep neural networks instead of back-propagation and gradient descent, but this discussion is not about this aspect of the usage of genetic algorithms. It's about how genetic algorithms can be used to evolve better deep neural networks. Anyway, if you're interested in how genetic algorithms can replace gradient-based optimization in advanced deep neural networks, you can read this paper: https://arxiv.org/abs/1712.06567.

The general framework for genetic algorithms is relatively simple. First, we generate a number of solutions to a problem and evaluate for each of them its performance. Then, we create a new generation of the solutions by crossing good solutions with each other from the previous generation, from time to time introducing some random mutations to increase variation. And we repeat this cycle until we have a reasonably appropriate solution to the problem.

Genetic algorithms can be used to evolve deep neural networks with optimal hyper-parameters. In this approach, we create a population of neural networks with different hyper-parameters and throw it in a genetic algorithm that will evolve a network with optimal hyper-parameters. Certainly, this is an extremely computationally expensive approach. But, reportedly, different systems of evolving deep neural networks using genetic algorithms are being used by some big companies.

Convolutional neural networks

Convolutional neural networks (CNNs or ConvNets) are a subcategory of feed-forward nets. For tasks in which repetitive patterns can be found – for example, it can be an image with repetitive edges and other patterns – CNNs are more computationally efficient than nonconvolutional feed-forward nets. Convolutional networks are particularly good at capturing local patterns in data due to the structure of convolutional layers.

Currently, the process of image recognition is implemented primarily by applying CNNs. Employing CNNs for image recognition in the 1990s was the first practical success of artificial neural networks. CNNs have already achieved superhuman performance at some image recognition tasks. These networks are also employed for a wide variety of other tasks, and these networks are the most frequently used type of deep neural networks today.

Convolutional networks usually have several hidden layers. But some convolutional networks have hundreds of hidden layers. Hidden layers that are closer to the input layer detect very simple features like edges and color gradients in the images. Then, the higher layers combine those simple features in more complex patterns. Finally, the layers that are close to the output combine those more complex patterns.

Interestingly, the structure of convolutional neural networks was initially inspired by studying the organization of the animal visual cortex. The concept of a *receptive field* – which is a link between parts of the visual fields and individual neurons in the brain – was particularly influential for creating convolutional networks.

You may be wondering why we need convolutional neural networks at all and why not just use fully connected networks.

Let's consider this situation. If we were to build a fully-connected network for image classification and work with say 300x300 px color images, the feature vector of this network would have 300x300x3 = 270.000 components. If the first hidden layer had 1000 neurons, this layer alone would have 1000x270.000 = 270.000.000 learnable parameters. The overall number of parameters in the entire network would likely be close to one billion. Neural networks with such a huge number of parameters are highly susceptible to overfitting. Moreover and even more importantly, such networks require a gargantuan amount of computational resources and time for training.

Convolutional neural networks have much fewer learnable parameters than fully-connected networks like the one in the above example, but the performance of CNNs is usually much better than that of fully-connected networks with the same number of neurons.

The fundamental component of any convolutional network is a *convolution operation*. Any neural network which has at least one layer that performs convolution operations is a convolutional network. A convolution operation does the element-wise product of a *filter* (also known as a *kernel*) in one region of an input. The input can be a vector, matrix, or multi-dimensional tensor.

Depending on what kind of filter is applied, we can have different results in the end. The size of a filter, as well as some other filter characteristics, is a hyper-parameter. Whereas, the values in a filter matrix are learnable parameters. The learning process in a convolutional neural network mostly consists of adjusting the values in filter matrices.

Before convolutional networks, the idea of filters was utilized in other algorithms for image processing. But filters in those algorithms were hand-crafted and didn't have learnable parameters.

In a convolutional layer, a filter slides over the input to this layer and performs a convolution operation:

1 a filter is lined up with a part of an image.

2 multiply each image pixel by the corresponding filter component

3 add them up

4 divide by the total number of filter components

5 apply a nonlinear activation function, which is usually ReLU

Then the filter moves to another position. This movement is defined by the *stride* of a convolutional layer. A stride determines how many components in the input we move the filter at a time.

Let me illustrate how convolution operations work with a simple toy example.

Let's say we have the following input:

1	-1	2	3
3	-1	3	1
0	-1	-1	3
3	3	1	0

And we have the following filter:

1	0
1	0

Now let's apply convolution operations to this input using this filter and a stride equal to 1:

1 x 1	-1x 0	2	3
3 x 1	-1x 0	3	1
0	-1	-1	3
3	3	1	0

→ 4

1	-1x 1	2 x 0	3
3	-1x 1	3 x 0	1
0	-1	-1	3
3	3	1	0

→ -2

1	-1	2 x 1	3 x 0
3	-1	3 x 1	1 x 0
0	-1	-1	3
3	3	1	0

→ 5

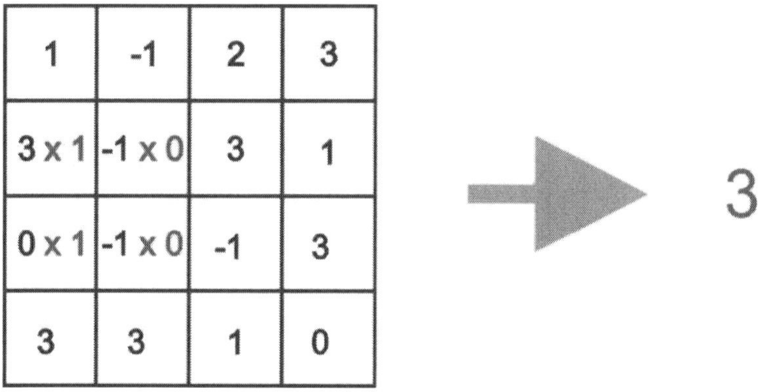

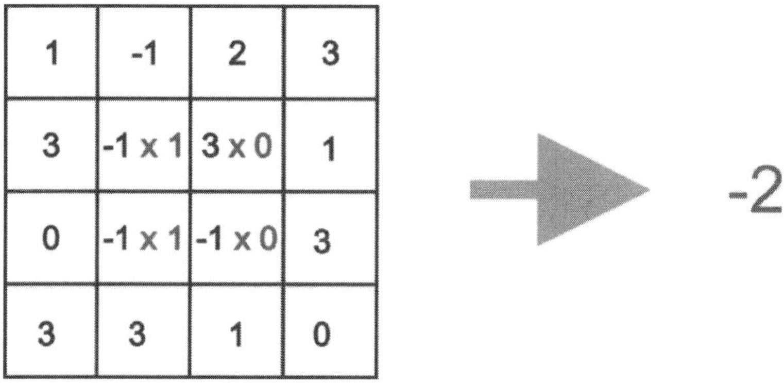

And so on all the way to the end...

And at the end, we have the following result (before applying an activation function to it):

4	-2	5
3	-2	2
3	2	0

By moving the filter to every possible position, we've produced a *feature map* of this filter.

Each filter represents a certain feature. A feature map shows how obvious this feature is at a certain position of the input.

As I said, a convolutional neural network has one or more convolutional layers. In a typical convolutional neural network, the last convolutional layer is flattened into one vector and usually fed into one or several fully-connected layers.

The majority of learnable parameters in most convolutional networks actually reside in their final fully-connected layers, not in convolutional layers. For example, in the famous AlexNet(2012) network, 59 million out of 62 million parameters were located in its final three fully connected layers. However, this tendency gradually changes with new architectures of CNNs.

The first and second dimensions of a convolutional layer are usually called height and width. The third dimension is referred to be as the number of channels.

One convolutional layer can – and usually does – have more than one filter. The output of a convolutional layer is a set of *activation* or *feature maps*. One filter produces one activation map. Each value in an activation map represents a value of one neuron.

The number of filters in one layer corresponds to the third dimension (the number of channels) of the output of this layer. The third dimension of a filter in a convolutional layer has to be equal to the number of activation maps from the previous layer.

Like in a simple fully-connected neural network, learnable parameters in convolutional neural networks consist of weights and biases. Each filter has the number of weights equal to the number of its components, and each filter can have one bias. In fact, the components of a filter are weights.

The output of a convolutional layer represents a vector if it's 1D convolution, a matrix if it's 2D convolution, or a tensor if it's a 3D convolution.

In the example above, we saw that we lost the size of the input in a convolutional layer.

The size of the output of a convolutional layer can be calculated by the following formula:

$$Output = (N - F)/stride + 1,$$

where

N – input size

F – filter size

For example, if we have a convolutional layer where the input is 30x30, filter is 4x4, and stride is 1, then we get

(30-4)/1+1=27

(30-4)/1+1=27.

Therefore the output will be 27x27.

The shrinking of the input size can become a problem when we have many convolutional layers in a neural network because each such a layer can reduce the input size.

In order to preserve the size of the input in a convolutional layer, we can use *padding*. Padding is adding a boarder around the edges of the input.

The most common type of padding is zero padding, which is just adding zero values, for example:

0	0	0	0	0	0
0	1	-1	2	3	0
0	3	-1	3	1	0
0	0	-1	-1	3	0
0	3	3	1	0	0
0	0	0	0	0	0

If we don't apply padding, not only do we lose the size, but also the pixels in the edges and corners are much less influence the output compared to the other pixels.

A typical convolutional network has not only convolutional and fully-connected layers. *Pooling layers* are also very common in ConvNets. A pooling layer shrinks the output of its previous layer. As such, pooling reduces computational requirements of a neural net. Similarly to a filter in a convolutional layer, a window in a pooling layer slides across the input. For example, if we use a filter size as 2 and stride as 2 in a pooling layer, this layer reduces the dimension of its previous layer output by a factor of 2.

There are different types of pooling layers: maximum pooling, average pooling, etc. Maximum pooling is the most common one. Maximum pooling just takes a maximum value in its window, for example:

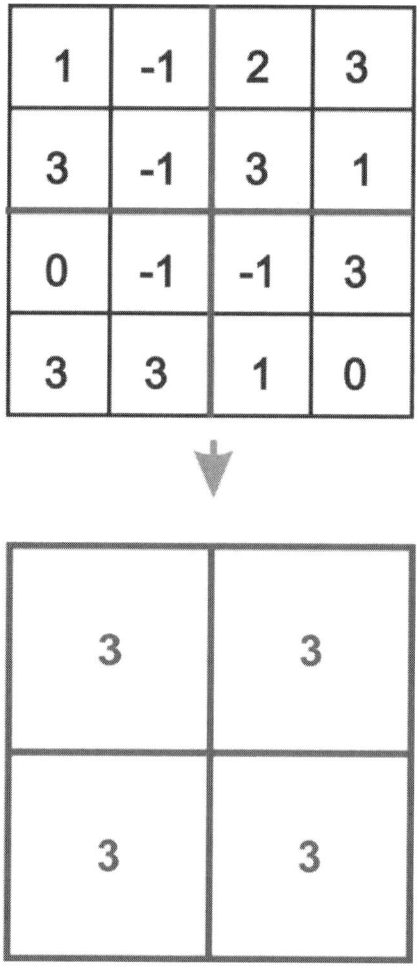

A pooling layer has no learnable parameters. Because of this, pooling layers are usually not included to the total number of layers of convolutional networks. For example, if a neural network has seven convolutional layers, three fully-connected layers, one soft-max layer, and four pooling layers, we say that this is an 11-layers deep neural network (7+3+1) because we only count layers with learnable parameters.

In some recent convolutional neural network architectures, fully-connected layers at the end of the networks are replaced by several average pooling layers. This allows these networks to drastically reduce the total number of learnable parameters in them, which leads to better overfitting prevention.

In addition to convolutional neural networks, there are also so-called *deconvolutional neural networks*. These networks utilize special operations called *deconvolutions* or *transposed convolutions*.

Deconvolutional neural networks usually use a method called *unpooling* or *unsampling* in their unpooling layers. Basically, it is the opposite of what pooling does. The output of an unpooling layer is an enlarged but sparse feature map. After unpooling, a deconvolutional network uses its deconvolutional layer. In this layer, the network densifies the sparse feature map coming from the unpooling layer using transposed convolutions. As a result, deconvolutional neural networks are able to increase image resolution or, speaking more generally, dimensionality of their inputs. Deconvolutional neural networks can be applied for generative models, for example.

The same effects of dimensionality input increasing that are provided by deconvolutional networks can be also achieved using convolutional networks with appropriate convolutional layers. So, we don't necessarily need to use deconvolutional neural networks. Also, often networks which have deconvolutional layers are simply called convolutional.

Recurrent Neural Networks

Both fully-connected and convolutional networks belong to feed-forward neural networks. This means that the signals in those networks move without making any loops inside the networks.

When we are working with neural networks, typically we have fix-sized inputs and fix-sized outputs. In fact, it was always the case for all our previous examples of neural networks. However, having fix-sized inputs and outputs impairs the execution of certain tasks. A classical example of such a task is translation. For performing adequate translation we need to have inputs and outputs of variable length. Moreover, convolutional and fully-connected networks do not take into account the order of their inputs, and this also becomes a serious problem for certain tasks.

There is a type of neural networks that doesn't have the limitations of feed-forward neural networks we just mentioned. These networks are called recurrent neural networks (RNNs). RNNs are especially good at dealing with sequential data. There are many various types of sequential data, for example, speech, video, various forms of time series. But RNNs can be also applied for non-sequential data as well, such as images.

It's also interesting that recurrent neural networks are much more similar to biological networks than feed-forward neural networks.

There are multiple variations of recurrent neural networks. The standard version of an RNN can be depicted as follows:

In this network, each hidden state receives the previous hidden state in addition to its direct input.

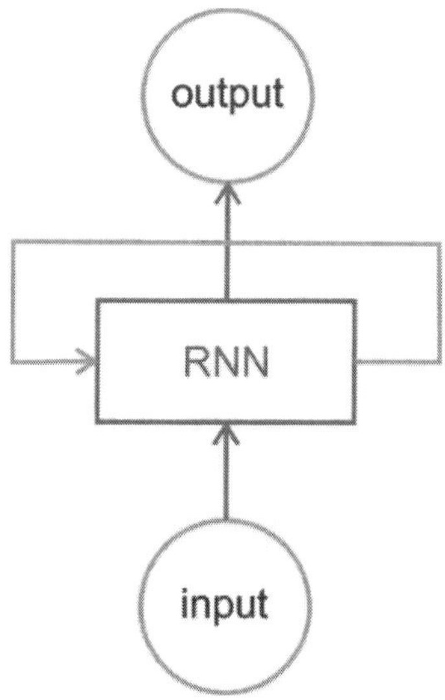

This representation of an RNN can be unfolded:

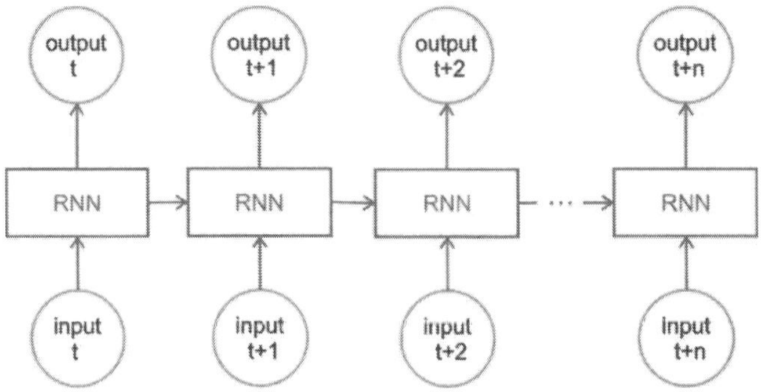

Of course, there is no yet previous hidden state for the first hidden state. So, we usually use zeros as the previous hidden state for the first hidden state, but there are other alternatives.

Note, that in this schema, all the vertical columns represent a single network, and this network gets a new input each time. In this case, we need to back-propagate all the way to the beginning of the sequence in order to find the gradients for the initial inputs. This process is called *backpropagation through time*. So, an RNN even with a single hidden layer can implement a tremendous amount of gradient multiplications, which often unwieldy or totally inefficient because the gradients either grow or vanish to zero exponentially.

This type of an RNN is rarely used these days. This standard version of an RNN is not very good at capturing long term dependencies in data, and it is highly vulnerable to the vanishing gradient problem.

There is a very popular architecture for RNNs called the long short-term memory network (LSTM). LSTM in its hidden layers has special computational units. Each such a unit can be viewed as several layers of neurons and some other operations combined together. LSTM networks usually outperform simple RNNs by a significant margin, because LSTM is not so vulnerable to the vanishing gradient problem and therefore able to learn long range dependencies

As opposed to a standard RNN unit, an LSTM unit has a memory cell, which can be also viewed as a pipe with data running through an entire hidden layer of LSTM.

An LSTM unit has three inputs:

1) input of the network or a previous hidden layer;

2) output of the previous LSTM unit state;

3) input of the memory cell

And it also has three outputs:

1) Output for the next LSTM unit state;

2) Output to the next layer (it coincides with the first output)
3) Output of the memory cell

An LSTM unit is quite complicated. The processes that take place in an LSTM unit can be described in the following equations:

$$f_t = \delta_g(W_f x_t + U_f h_{t-1} + b_f)$$

$$i_t = \delta_g(W_i x_t + U_i h_{t-1} + b_i)$$

$$o_t = \delta_g(W_o x_t + U_o h_{t-1} + b_o)$$

$$c_t = f_t \circ c_{t-1} + i_t \circ \delta_h(W_c x_t + U_c h_{t-1} + b_c)$$

$$h_t = o_t \circ \delta_g (c_t)$$

Where

x_t - input

h_{t-1} - output of the previous LSTM unit

f_t - forget gate

i_t – input gate

o_t – output gate

δ_g - sigmoid function

δ_h - hyperbolic tangent function

c_t – memory cell

h_t – output of the unit

W, U - weight matrices

b – biases

The forget gate determines to which extent the memory cell should forget its previous state. The input gate determines the extent to which an input flows into the memory cell. And the output gate controls the output of the LSTM unit.

From these equations, we see that the formulas for the forget, input, and output gates (f_t, i_t, o_t) are basically the same, but they have different parameters (W, U, b). All these three formulas have sigmoid functions in them. As you probably recall, a sigmoid function gives an output between 0 and 1. In these formulas, the sigmoid function serves as a valve or faucet by which a flow of the signals can be controlled.

I should say that you don't necessarily need to know these equations, as pretty much all the equations in this book, in order to be able to build and work with deep neural networks. Deep learning frameworks such as Keras allow us to build layers with LSTM units extremely easily, with a line of code.

Even though LSTM is much less susceptible to vanishing gradient than standard RNNs, LSTM networks have only several hidden layers. For example, reportedly, an LSTM network that is used in Google translation has only eight hidden layers. In addition to an LSTM unit, there is a similar alternative known as a gated recurrent unit (GRU).

An LSTM network can be combined with a CNN in one network. Such architectures can be used for image captioning and some other tasks. Also, a convolutional operation can be included in LSTM, or other RNN versions, itself.

Adversarial neural networks

So far, we've been mostly discussing *descriptive models*. A descriptive model learns a function that maps data samples with their labels. It can be classification or regression tasks of various forms. In descriptive models, the inputs are usually quite complicated, but outputs are very simple: it's a probability distribution for a classification task and a real number for a regression task.

However, we can invert this procedure and start getting complex outputs from more simple inputs, and this new approach is called *generative modeling*. Generative modeling is a type of unsupervised learning. There are several approaches to generative modeling in deep learning.

Deep generative models can produce amazing results in many domains. For example, some deep generative models are able to generate realistic-looking images or even videos from random noise. Moreover, given descriptions in natural language, some generative models can create or hallucinate unrealistic – and yet convincingly looking – images.

Some deep generative models are even used in chemical engineering to design new molecules of drugs and other chemicals.

Also, deep generative models can be used for simulating the future and environment in general for various tasks, including consecutive reinforcement learning. Generative models can be used for making synthetic data for other machine learning problems. There are plenty of other tasks where generative models can be applied.

There are different general deep neural network architectures that can be used in generative modeling. Both convolutional and recurrent neural networks can be applied for it. Also, there are so-called variational autoencoders and some other types of neural nets. But in this chapter, we'll be discussing another approach called Generative adversarial networks (GANs). GANs were originally proposed quite recently, in a 2014 paper by Ian Goodfellow and some other researchers from the University of Montreal (https://arxiv.org/pdf/1406.2661.pdf).

Four years later after their invention, there are a tremendous number of different variations of GANs. To get an idea how popular and versatile this approach has quickly become, you can check out this post: https://deephunt.in/the-gan-zoo-79597dc8c347.

A generative adversarial network consists of two separate neural networks: a discriminator and a generator.

These two networks compete with each other trying to outperform one another. This process is called *adversarial training*.

The generator generates samples of data usually given just vectors of random numbers.

The discriminator learns on a training set and then tries to find the difference between the real data from the training set and the fake ones generated by the generator.

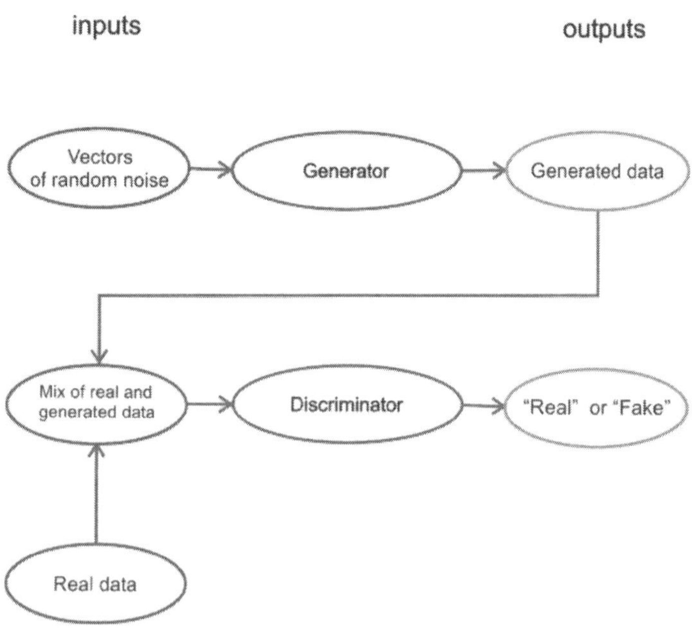

It's common to say that GANs belong to unsupervised learning. But to be more precise I should point out that a generative adversarial network is actually a mixture of supervised and unsupervised learning. A generator performs pure unsupervised learning, but a discriminator uses supervised learning because we tell the discriminator whether the image or some other type of input is real or fake. So, in this framework, we leverage supervised learning in order to improve unsupervised learning (a generative model).

In a typical GAN, a generator is a deconvolutional or convolutional network, and a discriminator is a convolutional network. If our task is generating images, the discriminator is just a typical binary image classifier (a convolutional neural network). But, as I said, there are a lot of various types of GANs for various tasks, which can use different neural network architectures. For example, recurrent networks can be also used in GANs for sound and video generation and many other tasks.

Let's discuss in more detail how a typical deep convolutional GAN (DCGAN) for image generation works.

In this architecture, the generator is given a vector of random numbers in its input layer which goes to the following fully-connected layer. Note that when we build convolutional nets for image classification, we don't use fully-connected layers at the beginning of the networks. In the generator, there are several convolutional layers after the fully-connected layer that gradually increase the dimensionality of the input. Such a network does not use max-pooling layers. Also, layers with transposed convolution can be applied in such a network. It's highly recommended to use the leaky ReLU activation function throughout the layers of the generator. However, in its final layer, it's most of the time recommended to use the hyperbolic tangent activation function. The final layer outputs images for the discriminator.

As I said, the discriminator is usually a standard convolutional network for binary classification. We train the discriminator first. In order to train the discriminator we need a training set containing similar images to the images we are going to generate. Of course, at this stage, the generator has not been trained yet and can produce only images consisting of random noise. So, the discriminator learns how to distinguish the target class images from random noise images. We can use some metric for supervised learning evaluation to evaluate the discriminator. After the discriminator has been trained and evaluated, the weights of the discriminator are frozen and no longer change.

After that, we can start training the generator. We train the generator until the discriminator can no longer distinguish between images from the data set and generated ones. So, the discriminator can only do random guessing when the GAN is trained.

In this framework, both the generator and discriminator use the same loss function. The discriminator tries to minimize this function, but the goal of the generator is to maximize this function.

Currently, deep convolutional GANs are able to generate the most realistic images among other generated models. And the scope of their other successful applications is growing. However, GANs are not easy to train to say the least.

It's very interesting that we can add to a model generated by a DCGAN a certain condition. For example, if we generate faces, we can add some additional features like glasses or beards to our generated images. In order to do so, we need to give a certain additional vector as an input to both the generator and discriminator. Also, we need to change the loss function. Such a network is called a Conditional

GAN. Another example of a conditional GAN can be a network that generates images given text descriptions. In this case, the images are generated from vectors consisting of random noise but conditioned by the text descriptions.

Deep reinforcement learning

Before jumping right into deep reinforcement learning, we should briefly discuss reinforcement learning in general.

Reinforcement learning (RL) is a quite complex topic, but at a high level of abstraction it can be viewed as a sequential decision-making process performed by an AI agent, where the agent learns which actions to take in order to achieve its goals, or, more precisely, to maximize its cumulative numeric reward. The agent always operates in some environment. It can be a virtual world of computer games or a real physical world, for example, in robotics. A reward is the feedback from the agent's environment that measures the agent's performance. It can be positive or negative. Whenever the agent takes a right action, it gets some positive expected reward. Also, rewards can be immediate or delayed.

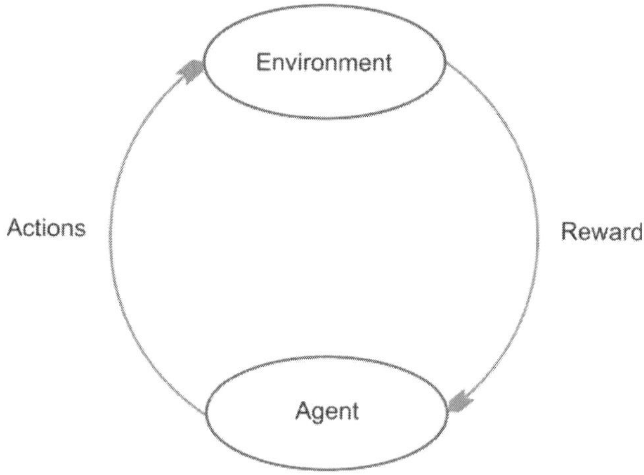

The agent is always in some state. For example, in robotics, it can be a physical state of the agent and its environment. Also, there are a finite number of time steps.

This book is not mathematically oriented, but, in this chapter, we will need quite a few samples of math formalism. I should say that although these math equations may look absolutely incomprehensible at first, actually this math is quite simple.

The agent constantly repeats the following cycle: state (S), action (A), reward (R) until the terminal state:

$$S_1 \rightarrow A_1 \rightarrow R_1 \rightarrow S_2 \rightarrow A_2 \rightarrow R_2 \rightarrow S_3 \rightarrow A_3 \rightarrow R_3 \rightarrow \ldots..$$

This whole sequence of states, actions and rewards or just any part of it is called a *trajectory*.

The agent has to have a strategy that determines which action to take in each state at each time step. In reinforcement learning, this strategy is called *policy* and usually denoted as $\boldsymbol{\pi}$.

A policy in reinforcement learning is a function of states that maps agent's states to actions. In reinforcement learning, our goal is to find the policy that maximizes the cumulative reward the agent receives. Such a policy is called the *optimal policy* $\boldsymbol{\pi}^*$. Also, a policy can be deterministic or probabilistic, and the latter option is usually the case.

In order to find the optimal policy we need to know which states or state-action pairs lead to the biggest cumulative reword. And this brings us to the *value function*.

The value function is a function of states or state-action pairs. This function estimates how good it is for the agent to be in a given state or take a given action in a given state in terms of the expected cumulative reward. A value function of state-action pairs is called the action-value function or *Q-function*. This function maps the state-action pairs to rewards. It's a little bit similar to supervised learning, but the distinctions are also significant.

The Q-function for a given policy can be written as the expected cumulative reword:

$$Q^{\pi}(s,a) = [r_t + \gamma r_{t+1} + \gamma^2 r_{t+2} + \dots + \gamma^n r_n]$$

Where

$\gamma - discount\ factor\ [0,1)$

In this equation, the subscripts ***t***, ***t+1 … n*** denote different time steps, and ***γ*** is a discount factor for future rewards, and ***γ*** is greater than 0 but less than 1, usually very close to 1, such as 0,9 or 0,99. So, ***γ*** with each time step makes future rewards slightly less valuable compared to the immediate reward r_t. It's similar to inflation in economics, where the purchasing power of money is gradually falling.

The Q-function for the optimal policy can be written as the *Bellman optimality equation*:

$$Q^*(s,a) = [r_t + \gamma \operatorname{argmax} Q^*(s',a')]$$

Where

r_t – $reward\ in\ the\ current\ state\ (immediate\ reward)$

$a - action\ in\ the\ current\ state$

$a' - actions\ in\ the\ following\ state$

$s - current\ state$

$s' - following\ state$

$Q - the\ value\ of\ being\ in\ a\ certain\ state/action$

$\gamma - discount\ factor$

In the *Bellman optimality equation*, there is a recursion. This equation means that the Q-value for a given state-action pair is equal to the reword for this particular state-action pair plus the Q-value for the next state-action pair multiplied by the discount factor.

In reinforcement learning problems, there is the so-called *exploration vs exploitation problem*. It turns out that taking only actions that maximize the Q-function when learning – it's called *greedy policy* – may prevent an agent from finding the best policy because the agent doesn't explore its environment completely. In this case, the agent gets stuck in a local minimum, so to speak. There are several ways to confront the exploration vs exploitation problem. The most common one is using a certain parameter **ε** in the Q-function. This parameter defines the probability of choosing a random action instead of following the agent's greedy policy. We start training with **ε** equal to 1. So, at the beginning, the agent only takes random actions and explores its environment. As the training progresses, **ε** is gradually decreasing. The rate of the **ε**-decrease is a hyper-parameter. When we're testing a reinforcement learning model or using it in production, we usually set the value for **ε** close to zero or zero. After incorporating the **ε** parameter, the Q-function for the optimal policy looks like this:

$$Q^*(s,a) = [r_t + \gamma\, \varepsilon \operatorname{argmax} Q^*(s', a')]$$

How are we going to solve the Bellman optimality equation? First of all, we could iterate through all possible state-actions pairs using dynamic programming. But this strategy is intractable for most real-world problems. Even for computer games or such games as Go, this strategy is not applicable either: there are always a tremendous number of possible scenarios. So, we should use some other strategy. And here machine learning comes into play.

It turns out that for simple problems, we can use some simple ML algorithms in order to approximate the Q-function and consequently find the optimal (or very close to optimal) policy. But we should use deep neural networks in order to do this for more complex tasks. Various methods of using machine learning algorithms to approximate the Q-function are collectively called *Q-learning*. And when we use a neural network as an ML algorithm in Q-learning, such a network is called a Q-network. The abbreviation DQN stands for a deep Q-network.

Q-learning iteratively updates a Q-function. In order to do Q-learning we need to construct a special type of Mean Squared Error loss function for an ML algorithm, which in our case is a neural network. This loss function can be written as:

$$\boldsymbol{L_i} = ([\boldsymbol{r_t} + \gamma\, \varepsilon\, \mathbf{argmax}\, \boldsymbol{Q}^*(\boldsymbol{s}', \boldsymbol{a}')] - \boldsymbol{Q}(\boldsymbol{s}, \boldsymbol{a}))^2$$

Where

$Q(s,a) - \ output\ of\ neural\ network$ *(estimated Q-value)*

We train a DQN by minimizing this loss function, and the loss function changes its state-actions pairs in each iteration i.

In a DQN, the final layer consists of neurons each of which corresponds to one possible action of the agent. But it isn't a classification neural network. Rather, it is more like a network for regression with multiple outputs. A DQN outputs the Q-values for each action. In each iteration, the DQN selects its maximum predicted Q-value.

For a long time, all attempts to approximate the Q-function with deep neural networks using raw sensory inputs had not been really successful. But in 2013, the group of researchers from DeepMind Technologies published the landmark paper, where they presented a convolutional neural network capable of learning policies directly from high-dimensional sensory inputs (it was screenshots) using reinforcement learning: *Playing Atari with Deep Reinforcement Learning* by V. Mnih et al. (https://arxiv.org/abs/1312.5602). They applied their network to seven Atari 2600 games, and the network surpassed a human expert on three of the games. It was a phenomenal result. Later the researchers from DeepMind applied the same model to other Atari games and again obtained outstanding results.

It was a quite simple convolutional network that only had three convolutional and two fully-connected hidden layers. The network didn't have any pooling layers.

There were three major hacks or additions that allowed the DQN for playing Atari games to perform exceptionally well compared to previous neural networks for reinforcement learning.

The first innovation was *experience replay*. The researchers created a special memory buffer for storing an agent's experiences, which were stored as trajectories of a fixed size. From that buffer, the DQN occasionally received its previous experiences chosen randomly. In this setting, the DQN could learn much longer and probably less obvious relations between various state-action pairs.

The second really important thing was creating one additional neural network: the target Q-network. So, there were two separate neural networks with the same architecture: the online Q-network and the target Q-network. The online Q-network selects the action for a given state, and from the target Q-network we get the Q-value of that action. The online Q-network implements back-propagation and updates its parameters in each iteration of the training process. But the target Q-network updates its parameters only once in about 1.000 iterations, so the target Q-network gets more robust to immediate variations in training.

Finally, the researchers normalized all the rewards to the values in the interval between -1 to 1. Also, the gradients were normalized as well. These normalizations proved to be extremely important for stabilizing the network's performance.

The DQN for playing Atari games was the first major success of deep reinforcement learning that sparked the interest of many researchers and programmers throughout the world. Recently, there have been other successful approaches to deep reinforcement learning, in addition to Q-learning.

Remember a policy is a function of states that outputs actions. It turns out that instead of approximating the Q-function we can approximate a policy function itself. This approach is called policy-based reinforcement learning.

In Atari games, there are several joystick positions and one button, so there is a perfectly discrete action-space. But there are many tasks, where agents operate in a continues or almost continues action spaces. For example, a robot can have multiple joints which move in a continuous manner. Policy-based reinforcement learning especially comes in handy in such tasks.

There are different variations of policy-based reinforcement learning algorithms. One group of such algorithms combines policy-based reinforcement learning with Q-learning. This group represents the so-called *Actor–Critic Methods*. An actor-critic method or algorithm consists of two neural networks: the actor and the critic. The actor network outputs desirable actions for an RL agent in a continuous action space. The critic gets the actions predicted by the actor and outputs the Q-values of these actions. So, the critic is a standard DQN network.

An actor-critic algorithm was used for playing Go in the famous computer program *AlphaGo* developed by Google DeepMind. Go is a board game with incredible complexity. There are 2,1 x 10^{170} possible board positions in Go. It's an incredibly large number. For this reason, Go had long been considered unamendable to AI methods. But in 2016, the team of researchers from DeepMind published a seminal paper, where they presented the AlphaGo program that had defeated the human European Go champion by 5 games to 0: *Mastering the game of Go with deep neural networks and tree search* by D. Silver et al.

(https://www.nature.com/articles/nature16961). It was another amazing feat of reinforcement learning.

However, AlphaGo uses not only just deep reinforcement learning. Another critical component of AlphaGo is Monte Carlo tree search. By the way, various search algorithms such as Monte Carlo tree search are extremely important methods of classical AI, but such algorithms do not belong to machine learning.

In 2017, the researchers from DeepMind published another landmark paper where they presented an even better deep reinforcement learning architecture for playing Go: *Mastering the Game of Go without Human Knowledge* by D. Silver et al.

Deep reinforcement learning is still usually a research area. Now, deep RL is mostly applied to computer games, which means that now most RL agents operate only in strictly limited virtual world environments. However, reinforcement learning also starts making forays into more practical areas such as robotics and conversational AI agents.

And reinforcement learning is very promising. Some experts in this field believe that reinforcement learning is key to creating AI agents capable of performing a wide range of various tasks, as opposed to current AI applications, which are extremely narrow. Some even think that deep reinforcement learning is a direct road to creating artificial general intelligence.

However, there are many problems in reinforcement learning that need to be solved for building really intelligent agents. In particular, in many tasks for reinforcement learning, the major rewards are extremely delayed or sparse. For example, in such games as chess, checkers, or Go, the agent gets its major reward only at the end of the game. Similar situations can be found not just in games but in other tasks for reinforcement learning as well. For example, a robot may have to perform a lot of prior individual manipulations in order to accomplish its target task. This is known as *sparse rewards problem*, and it's one of the biggest problems in reinforcement learning. The sparse rewards problem causes another problem known as the *credit assignment problem*. The credit assignment problem refers to the situation when it's very difficult to determine which particular prior action has contributed to receiving the major reward the most.

There are even harder and apparently more profound problems in reinforcement learning. For example, such problems include combining reinforcement learning with memory and efficient unsupervised learning. In virtual world environments, we can always start over the learning processes of RL agents. But in the tasks where RL agents operate in physical world environments, these RL robotic agents tend to make fatal mistakes for themselves soon or later – sometimes very quickly – if they use only RL in their learning procedures. Instead, if the agents could acquire part of the knowledge about their environments by pure observation without physical interactions with the physical world and then use this knowledge for accomplishing their tasks, they would avoid making many mistakes and, apparently, learn much better.

Part II Introduction to Building Neural Networks with Keras

Introduction to Keras

Modern deep neural networks are quite complex structures that often have incredibly large numbers of components. It may look like that it takes much effort to code such structures. But modern libraries for deep learning allow us to build, train, and use deep neural networks much easier than ever before.

As you probably noticed, I've mentioned the Keras library several times throughout this book, and there is a good reason for that. Currently, Keras is probably the most intuitive, easy-to-use, and yet remarkably flexible and powerful API for deep learning. Keras is written in Python, which is another advantage. Recently, this API has become one the most popular APIs for building neural networks. Keras can be deployed on top of three frameworks for deep learning: TensorFlow, Theano, and Microsoft Cognitive Toolkit (CNTK). According to Keras documentation, it is recommended to use the TensorFlow backend. This means we need one of these frameworks being installed to install and be able to work with Keras. However, latest versions of TensorFlow contain Keras in them already. So, we can simply use the latest version of TensorFlow and import Keras from it in our scripts for deep learning. And we're going to use this strategy in this chapter. So, I highly recommend you visit https://www.tensorflow.org/guide/keras. Also, I highly recommend checking Keras official documentation: https://keras.io. In this chapter, I'll show how to build some neural network architectures using this excellent API for deep learning.

By the way, in order to use Keras efficiently, in most cases, you don't have to be an experienced Python programmer. Keras is much easier than pure TensorFlow. If you want instead to use the TensorFlow API for deep learning, you probably need to know Python better. In addition, not only is Keras easier, but it also allows building neural networks significantly faster than pure TensorFlow. So, I highly recommend using Keras.

Now, let's briefly discuss the hardware for deep learning. When we use our computers, usually the CPUs inside them implement the majority of computational operations. A CPU is usually designed for implementing quite complex operations. It can, of course, do some simple operations like addition or multiplication of two numbers, but modern CPUs are not really designed for that kind of activity. On the contrary, some GPUs, can have hundreds of cores, and can significantly speed up implementation of simple computational operations, such as algebraic operations in neural networks, although GPUs are not able to do all the amazing stuff what CPUs can perform with the same efficiency.

In particular, some recent models of NVIDIA GPUs (https://developer.nvidia.com/cuda-gpus) can be operated through a special software layer called CUDA (Compute Unified Device Architecture), which allows them to efficiently perform general-purpose processing operations remarkably easy for us, users, compared to some other previous methods. The appearance of this technology has been one of the major factors for most achievements in applied deep learning in recent years. Working with deep learning models on a proper GPU gives a speedup advantage by a factor of 10, and usually even more, compared to doing deep learning on a CPU.

So, if you're really serious about deep learning, you should probably have some GPU which is appropriate for this purpose. In addition to having a right GPU, you need to install CUDA on your computer from NVIDIA's website. If you use Windows, you also need to install Visual Studio. Keras supports CUDA, and we don't even need to change the code of our neural networks whether we want to run them on a CPU or GPU. Most examples of neural networks in this chapter can be efficiently executed on a CPU. However, one of the examples is more suited for a GPU, but it can also be implemented on a CPU. Of course, the training process will take a longer time in this case.

The good news is that if you don't have an appropriate GPU for deep learning or required packages installed on your computer, you can still work with quite big deep learning models. You can use major paid cloud computer services such as Microsoft Azure, Amazon AWS, Google Cloud Platform, or IBM Cloud. But using such services on a regular basis can be quite expensive. There is also a good free option called Google Colaboratory (or Google Colab): https://colab.research.google.com, which comes with built-in TensorFlow and Keras both for CPU and GPU environments, and it also allows users to train deep models on a TPU. In order to be able to use Google Colab you just need to have the Chrome web-browser, a Google account, and a Google drive account. But be aware that the GPU and TPU versions of Google Colab often work not very reliably, especially in certain countries. Anyway, the CPU version can be a very good option for you, especially if you're a beginner.

When we're building and working with neural networks, oftentimes we need some other indispensable libraries for data science. If you want to code your own deep neural networks, I highly recommend downloading the Anaconda platform for data science: https://www.anaconda.com/download. It's free. It can be used on Linux, Windows, and macOS. Anaconda is a standard option for doing data science nowadays, especially for those who don't want to search for and download countless packages separately. Moreover, Anaconda has preinstalled Jupyter Notebook. Jupyter Notebook is a web-application that allows building live and interactive scripts just inside a web-browser. Jupyter Notebook is also a standard for doing data science in Python these days. The latest version of Anaconda has 1.8 TensorFlow. Also, Anaconda includes Python, so we don't have to install Python separately if we have Anaconda installed. When you download Anaconda chose the version with 3.6 Python unless you're more familiar with 2.7 Python.

Once you download Anaconda and launch Anaconda Navigator on your computer, you can launch a Jupyter Notebook. In order to do this, click the bottom like shown in the picture below:

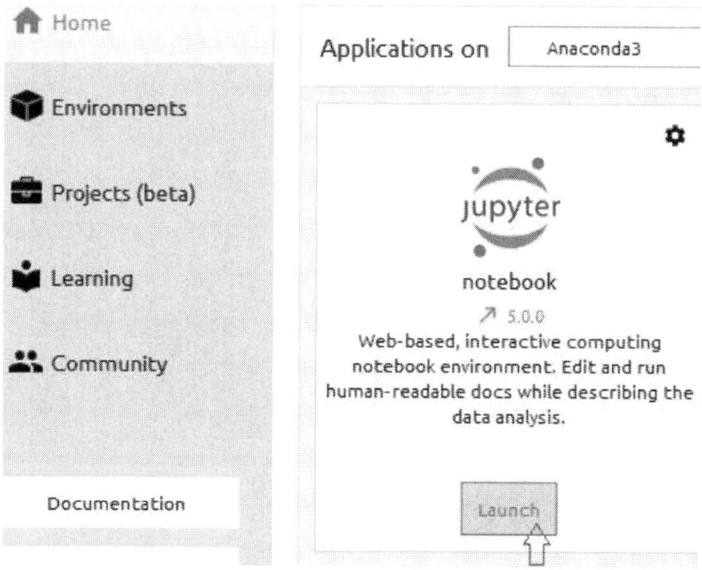

In a few seconds, your browser should open up with the Jupyter Notebook. Then you can create a new document as shown:

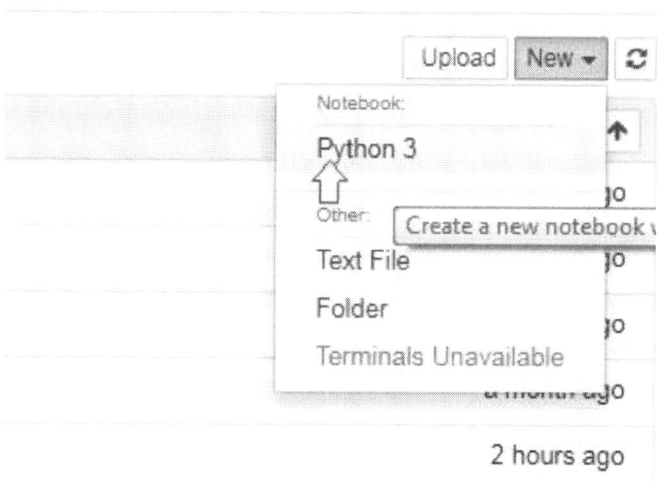

Congratulations! Now you can start building your own awesome deep neural networks. And, maybe it's easier than you think. So, let's get started.

A simple deep neural network for classification

Our first neural network is going to be a network for multiclass classification.

First thing first, we should import the packages we need for this task:

```
from tensorflow.keras.models import Sequential

from tensorflow.keras.layers import Dense, Activation

from tensorflow.keras.datasets import mnist

from tensorflow.keras.utils import normalize, to_categorical

import numpy as np
```

Keras provides two types of models for constructing neural networks: sequential and functional. Sequential modes are perhaps a little bit more intuitive than the functional ones. So, let's build a simple neural network for classification as a sequential model in Keras. This network contains three hidden layers with ReLU and one output layer with the softmax function.

We can define this network by using the **add** method:

```
model = Sequential()
#first hidden layer
model.add(Dense(128, activation='relu',
input_shape=(784,)))
#second hidden layer
model.add(Dense(128, activation='relu'))
#third hidden layer
model.add(Dense(64, activation='relu'))
#output layer
model.add(Dense(10, activation='softmax'))
```

Or we can define this network like this:

```
model = Sequential([
Dense(128,  input_shape=(784,)),
Activation('relu'),
Dense(128),
Activation('relu'),
```

```
Dense(64),

Activation('relu'),

Dense(10),

Activation('softmax')

])
```

These two pieces of code are equivalent. We need to specify the numbers of neurons in the layers and the types of the layers. As you can see, in this simple model, we use **Dense** layers. Keras also provides other types of layers, such as different types of convolutional layers. In the layers, we can also specify methods of parameter initialization, but we use the default parameter initialization. In the layers, we could also apply regularization methods.

A Keras model needs to know its input dimension. So, we need to define the input dimension in the first layer. Keras allows us to do this in several different ways (https://keras.io/getting-started/sequential-model-guide/#specifying-the-input-shape). In the following layers after the first hidden one, the model recognizes the input dimensions automatically.

Keras uses no activation function as a default parameter, so we need to define which type of activation function is applied, which is ReLU in our example. However, according to Keras documentation, ReLU in Keras is actually a version of the LeakyReLU activation function, but it doesn't impair our model, of course. You can check activation functions available in Keras yourself.

After building the model, we should compile this model by calling the **compile** method:

```
model.compile(optimizer='adam',
          loss='categorical_crossentropy',
          metrics=['accuracy'])
```

In the **compile** method, we need to define the optimization algorithm (we use Adam), the loss function, and the metric for evaluation.

Of course, we have to define our training dataset. In this example, we're using a standard dataset for image classification with neural networks: the MNIST dataset of handwritten digits. This dataset consists of two sub-sets (training and testing sets) consisting of 60.000 and 10.000 28x28 pixel grayscale images of 10 digits. This dataset is included both in Keras and TensorFlow, but you can also find it on some web resources for data scientists like Kaggle. In this example, we use the dataset from Keras to make our work easier.

```
(x_train, y_train), (x_test, y_test) = mnist.load_data()
```

I should point out that the data we have downloaded are represented as Numpy arrays or tensors. So, we can manipulate this data with the help of Numpy methods. And any data for working with Keras must be represented in the form of Numpy arrays.

In this example, we normalize the data applying the **normalize** method so that all values fall in the interval of 0 to 1. It turns out that this is an extremely important procedure for this task. Doing this task, I tried different optimization algorithms and different configurations of the network, but nothing of those worked very well without normalizing the data. In addition, we need to convert our dependant vectors into categorical labels, by using the **to_categorical** method:

```
x_train = normalize(x_train, axis=1)

x_test =  normalize(x_test, axis=1)

y_train = to_categorical(y_train, num_classes=None)
```

```
y_test = to_categorical(y_test, num_classes=None)
```

Then, we need to set aside one more separate test for validating our model. And we split our training test into two ones:

```
x_val = x_train[:10000]

partial_x_train = x_train[10000:]

y_val = y_train[:10000]

partial_y_train = y_train[10000:]
```

As a result, now we have three tests: the training set consisting of 50.000 samples, the validating set consisting of 10.000 samples, and the testing set also consisting of 10.000 samples.

Also, we need to reshape our 28x28 pixel images into 784x1 vectors. For this purpose, we use the **reshape** method:

```
partial_x_train = partial_x_train.reshape(50000, 784)

x_val = x_val.reshape(10000, 784)
```

```
x_test = x_test.reshape(10000, 784)

partial_x_train = partial_x_train.astype('float32')

x_val = x_val.astype('float32')

x_test = x_test.astype('float32')
```

Now we should compile our model by using the compile method:

```
model.compile (optimizer='adam',
loss='categorical_crossentropy', metrics=['accuracy'])
```

In this method, we define the optimization algorithm, loss function, and metric for our model.

Finally, we can train our model. In order to do this, we need to call the **fit** method. If you're familiar with the Scikit-Learn library, you may notice that this Keras method is similar to the **fit** method from Scikit-Learn. In the **fit** method, we define our training data, our validating data, the number of epochs, the **verbose** parameter (it simply determines the way the result will be shown):

```
model.fit(partial_x_train, partial_y_train,
        validation_data=(x_val, y_val),
        epochs=3, verbose=2)
```

```
Train on 50000 samples, validate on 10000 samples
Epoch 1/3
 - 23s - loss: 0.2888 - acc: 0.9127 - val_loss: 0.1409 - val_acc: 0.958
Epoch 2/3
 - 14s - loss: 0.1174 - acc: 0.9637 - val_loss: 0.1104 - val_acc: 0.968
Epoch 3/3
 - 25s - loss: 0.0809 - acc: 0.9742 - val_loss: 0.1069 - val_acc: 0.968
```

As you see, we train our model for just 3 epochs and get about 97% accuracy, which is pretty good for a neural network with no convolutional layers.

In the **fit** method, we could also specify the parameters of the optimization algorithms such as the learning rate, and we could specify the batch size.

In this example, we split our dataset into training and validating sets beforehand. But we could split it right inside the **fit** method by using the parameter **validation_split**. It's very convenient.

After training, we should evaluate our model on the testing data by using the **evaluate** method:

```
model.evaluate(x_test, y_test)
```

```
10000/10000 [==============================] - 2s
[0.10801190516538918, 0.9689]
```

After training and evaluating, we can use the **predict** method on new data.

As you can see, the general workflow for building and using neural networks in Keras consists of these major steps:

1 define the training, evaluating(optionally), and testing data;

2 define the neural network structure (model);

3 compile the model;

4 train and validate the model;

5 evaluate the model;

6 predict on new data.

We can also save Keras models by applying the **save** method:

```
model.save('model.h5')
```

In this method, we have to specify the name and the format of the file. We use the HDF5 format. There are different ways of saving models in Keras. We can either save only a model’s structure without its weights or a model’s structure with weights. In this example, we’ve saved our model with its weights. So, next time we won’t need to train this model again.

After saving the model, we can load this model whenever we need by applying the **load_model** method:

```
model = keras.models.load_model('model.h5')
```

We can also call the **summary** function to get general information about our model:

```
model.summary()
```

```
Layer (type)                 Output Shape              Param #
=================================================================
dense_8 (Dense)              (None, 128)               100480
_________________________________________________________________
activation_8 (Activation)    (None, 128)               0
_________________________________________________________________
dense_9 (Dense)              (None, 128)               16512
_________________________________________________________________
activation_9 (Activation)    (None, 128)               0
_________________________________________________________________
dense_10 (Dense)             (None, 64)                8256
_________________________________________________________________
activation_10 (Activation)   (None, 64)                0
_________________________________________________________________
dense_11 (Dense)             (None, 10)                650
_________________________________________________________________
activation_11 (Activation)   (None, 10)                0
=================================================================
Total params: 125,898
Trainable params: 125,898
Non-trainable params: 0
```

As you can see, our model has 125.898 learnable parameters, most of which are located in the first hidden layer.

Introduction to the functional API in Keras

Although sequential models in Keras are very intuitive, they are quite limited in what they can do. But Keras also provides functional models. Remember that each layer in a neural network can be viewed as a function? And this is the essence of functional models in Keras.

In a functional model, each layer is represented as a function with its input and output.

Every sequential model in Keras can be converted into a functional one, but not all functional models can be converted into sequential.

Let's convert our sequential model we just built into a functional modal:

```
from tensorflow.keras.models import Model

from tensorflow.keras.layers import Input, Dense, Activation

from tensorflow.keras.datasets import mnist

from tensorflow.keras.utils import normalize, to_categorical

import numpy as np

inputs = Input(shape=(784,))
```

```
x = Dense(128, activation='relu')(inputs)

x = Dense(128, activation='relu')(x)

x = Dense(64, activation='relu')(x)

outputs = Dense(10, activation='softmax')(x)

model = Model(inputs, outputs)
```

All the other steps in this functional model starting from downloading the dataset are exactly the same as in the sequential model. In my opinion, Keras functional models are also very intuitive.

Functional models are much more flexible than sequential ones. There are several major ways how we can use functional models to build more complex and more powerful neural networks.

First of all, with using the functional API, we can construct neural networks that have internal branching between their hidden layers. Such a network can be viewed as a graph and may look like this:

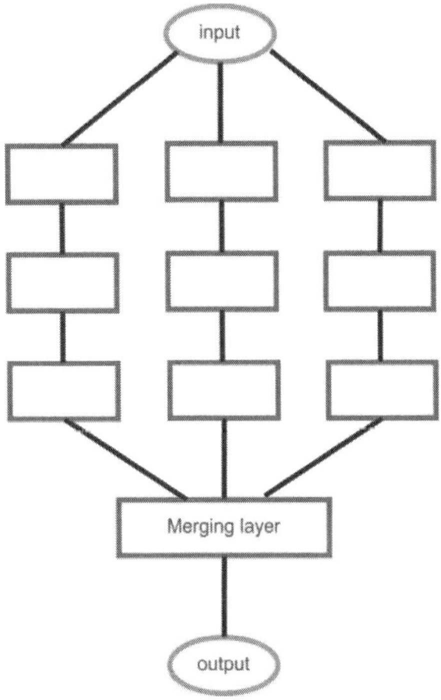

The functional API can be used, for instance, for building *residual* and *inception deep neural networks*, which are advanced types of convolutional networks. I didn't cover them in this introduction, but if you want, you can read about them in the original papers: https://arxiv.org/abs/1512.03385 and https://arxiv.org/abs/1409.4842.

In addition to building networks with internal branching between their layers, the functional API allows us to use layers from one model in other models. Also, with the functional API, we can even treat an entire model as a single layer for another model.

Using the functional API, we can construct networks that have multiple inputs and/or outputs. For example, a neural network can have inputs of different data types such as text, image, video etc. Then these multimodal vectors are concatenated in the merging modules of the network. For instance, a visual question answering model which answers natural-language questions about pictures or videos can be built in this way. Or given information from social media accounts, we can build a network with several outputs, such as user's age, gender, ext; this is one of many possible examples of many-outputs models which can be built with the Keras functional API. Models with multiple input-outputs are also prevalent in modern creative applications of deep learning (some architectures of GANs), and they also can be built using the functional API.

So, when we want to build an advanced neural network with Keras, in most cases the functional API is our choice.

Regression with Keras

Now let's build a neural network for regression. As you probably remember, a neural network for regression problems outputs just one single number, so the output layer has only one neuron.

Keras contains a dataset for regression – it's called the *Boston housing price regression dataset* – and we're going to work with this dataset in our network for regression. According to Keras documentation, the data samples in this dataset have 13 attributes of houses at different locations around the Boston suburbs in the late 1970s. The labels are the median values of the houses at a location. This dataset is quite small and has only 506 data samples which are split between 404 training samples and 102 test samples.

Again, it is going to be a quite simple neural network, but we will be training this network for a larger number of epochs than the one from the previous example because now we have much fewer data samples for training. So, let's get started.

As always, we import the packages we need:

```
from tensorflow.keras.models import Model

from tensorflow.keras.layers import Input, Dense, Activation

from tensorflow.keras.datasets import boston_housing

from sklearn.model_selection import KFold

from tensorflow.keras import initializers

import matplotlib.pyplot as plt

import pandas as pd

import numpy as np
```

then download the dataset:

```
(x_train, y_train), (x_test, y_test) =
boston_housing.load_data()
```

Using *Pandas*, which is by the way another awesome library for data science, we can display our data samples in a table:

```
df = pd.DataFrame(x_train)

df.round(2).head()
```

As a result we see the first five data samples from the dataset:

	0	1	2	3	4	5	6	7	8	9	10	11	12
0	1.23	0.0	8.14	0.0	0.54	6.14	91.7	3.98	4.0	307.0	21.0	396.90	18.72
1	0.02	82.5	2.03	0.0	0.42	7.61	15.7	6.27	2.0	348.0	14.7	395.38	3.11
2	4.90	0.0	18.10	0.0	0.63	4.97	100.0	1.33	24.0	666.0	20.2	375.52	3.26
3	0.04	0.0	5.19	0.0	0.52	6.04	34.5	5.99	5.0	224.0	20.2	396.90	8.01
4	3.69	0.0	18.10	0.0	0.71	6.38	88.4	2.57	24.0	666.0	20.2	391.43	14.65

As you can see, different features have different ranges of values. This can significantly hurdle the training process as the features with larger values will overweight other features. We can normalize or standardize (some other terminology is also used) this heterogeneous data using the following code:

```
mean = x_train.mean(axis=0)

std = x_train.std(axis=0)

x_train = (x_train - mean) / std

x_test = (x_test - mean) / std
```

In this code, we compute the mean and standard deviation for each feature in the training data. Then from each data sample feature in the training and testing datasets we subtract the mean and divide by the standard deviation.

After normalizing, these data samples look like this:

	0	1	2	3	4	5	6	7	8	9	10	11	12
0	-0.27	-0.48	-0.44	-0.26	-0.17	-0.18	0.81	0.12	-0.63	-0.60	1.15	0.45	0.83
1	-0.40	2.99	-1.33	-0.26	-1.22	1.89	-1.91	1.25	-0.86	-0.35	-1.72	0.43	-1.33
2	0.12	-0.48	1.03	-0.26	0.63	-1.83	1.11	-1.19	1.68	1.57	0.78	0.22	-1.31
3	-0.40	-0.48	-0.87	-0.26	-0.36	-0.32	-1.24	1.11	-0.51	-1.09	0.78	0.45	-0.65
4	-0.01	-0.48	1.03	-0.26	1.33	0.15	0.69	-0.58	1.68	1.57	0.78	0.39	0.26

Due to the scarcity of the training data, we will not set aside a separate single validating set in this example. Instead, we're going to use a method for cross-validation from the scikit-learn machine learning library.

So, here is some code to peruse:

```
#setting up a seed value for reproducibility of the results
seed = 0
np.random.seed(seed)
# cross validation method from scikit-learn
```

```
kf = KFold(n_splits=3, shuffle=True, random_state=seed)

cvscores = []

#weights initializer

init = initializers.glorot_uniform(seed=0)

#loop for cross validation

for train, test in kf.split(x_train, y_train):

    inputs = Input(shape=(13, ))

    layer1 = Dense(64, activation='relu', kernel_initializer =
init,

    bias_initializer = 'Ones')(inputs)

    layer2 = Dense(32, activation='relu', kernel_initializer =
init,

    bias_initializer = 'Ones')(layer1)

    layer3 = Dense(32, activation='relu', kernel_initializer =
init,

    bias_initializer = 'Ones')(layer2)

    outputs = Dense(1, kernel_initializer = init,

    bias_initializer = 'Ones')(layer3)

    model = Model(inputs, outputs)

    model.compile(loss='mse', optimizer='adam',
metrics=['mae'])
```

```
    model.fit(x_train, y_train, epochs=200, verbose=0)

    scores=model.evaluate(x_test, y_test, verbose=0)

    print(model.metrics_names[1], np.round(scores[1],
decimals=3), "$")

    cvscores.append(scores[1])

print("MAE: ", np.round(np.mean(cvscores), decimals=3),
"$" ,";"

    ,"(","+/-", np.round(np.std(cvscores), decimals=3), "$",
")" )
```

As you see, we define, compile, and evaluate our model inside a for loop. Of course, we could define the exact same network using the sequential API, but I deliberately applied the functional API in this example to help you get used to the API which is far more flexible. Notice that the **inputs** is the input for the first hidden layer; in turn the output of the first hidden layer (**layer1**) is the input for the second hidden layer and so on.

In this example, we use the **glorot_uniform** weights initializer with a fixed value of seed for the sake of reproducibility of our results.

This is a simple neural network with three hidden layers with 64 and 32 weights. In this task, we don't have much training data, so if the network had much more learnable parameters, it would be highly susceptible to overfitting.

In this example, we use the same optimization algorithm, which is **adam**, as in the previous network. But this is a regression problem, so we use a different loss function and metric. The loss function for this task is the mean squared error (**mse**), and the metric is the mean absolute error (**mae**).

When we execute that code, we get the following output:

```
mean_absolute_error 2.298 $
mean_absolute_error 2.259 $
mean_absolute_error 2.251 $
MAE:  2.269 $ ; ( +/- 0.02 $ )
```

As you see, we make a mistake of 2.269 $ on average. It's not bad for this particular task with little training data.

We can also plot our results using the **predict** method with the test data:

```
test_predictions  = model.predict(x_test).flatten()

test_predictions = test_predictions * 1000
```

```
y_test = y_test * 1000

plt.scatter(y_test, test_predictions)

plt.xlabel('True Values $')

plt.ylabel('Predictions $')

plt.xlim(plt.xlim())

plt.ylim(plt.ylim())

plt.show()
```

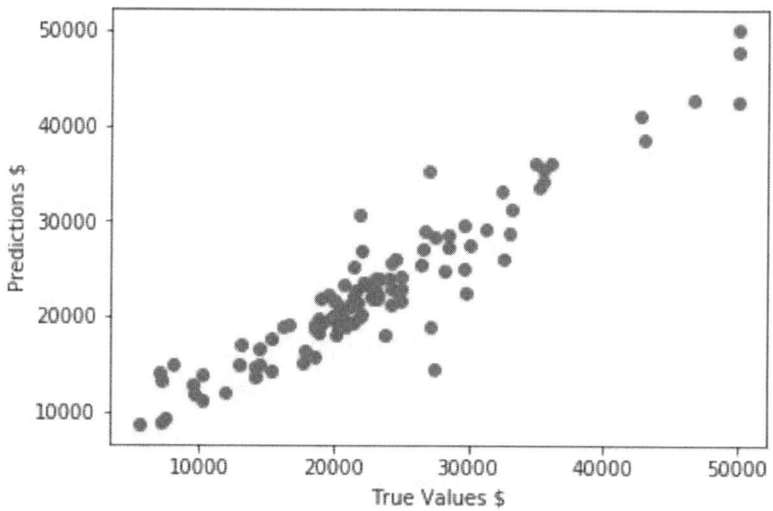

Keras Callbacks

So far, in the examples, we have been given the performance of our models only at the end of the trainings. But wouldn't it be great if we could see what's going on inside of our models during different phases of training? It would allow us to choose the optimal number of epochs for training and make much less effort to tune the models much better. The good news is we can easily do it with Keras. It especially comes in handy and even becomes absolutely necessary when we're dealing with very large and complex models because training such models can take a very long time, sometimes several weeks.

Keras provides us with callbacks. In Keras, a callback is a set of functions which can be applied at different stages of training. There are many types of different callbacks. In particular, there is a callback that records the performance of internal stages of a Keras model into the **History** object. This callback is applied automatically to every model. The **History** object gets returned by the **fit** method.

Let's see how we can use the **History** object in our neural network for classification.

But now let's train the network for 20 epochs. Of course, this time the training will take longer. Also, we should put **model.fit()** in a separate variable. The rest of the code remains unchanged:

```
hist=model.fit(partial_x_train, partial_y_train,
        validation_data=(x_val, y_val),
        epochs=20, verbose=0)
```

Then, we can plot the values of the loss function during different stages of training using this code:

```
import matplotlib.pyplot as plt
plt.title('Training and validation loss')
plt.plot(hist.history['loss'], label='Training loss')
plt.plot(hist.history['val_loss'], label='Validation loss')
plt.xlabel('Epochs')
plt.ylabel('Loss')
plt.legend()
plt.show()
```

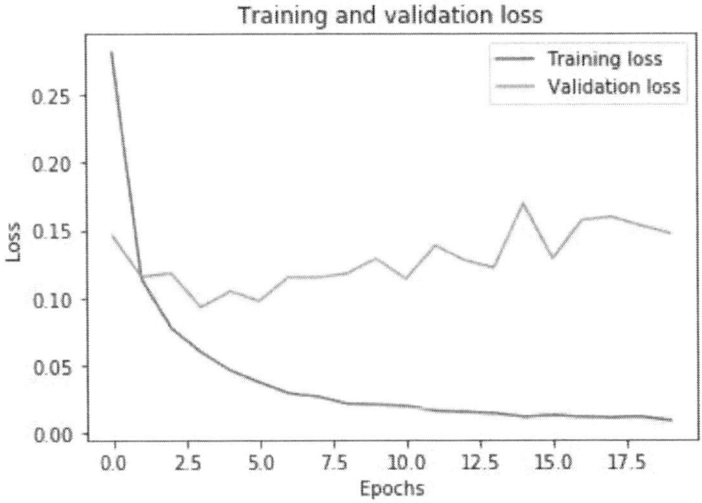

The same we can do for the metrics:

```
plt.title('Training and validation accuracy')

plt.plot(hist.history['acc'], label='Training accuracy')

plt.plot(hist.history['val_acc'], label='Validation accuracy')

plt.xlabel('Epochs')

plt.ylabel('Accuracy')

plt.legend()

plt.show()
```

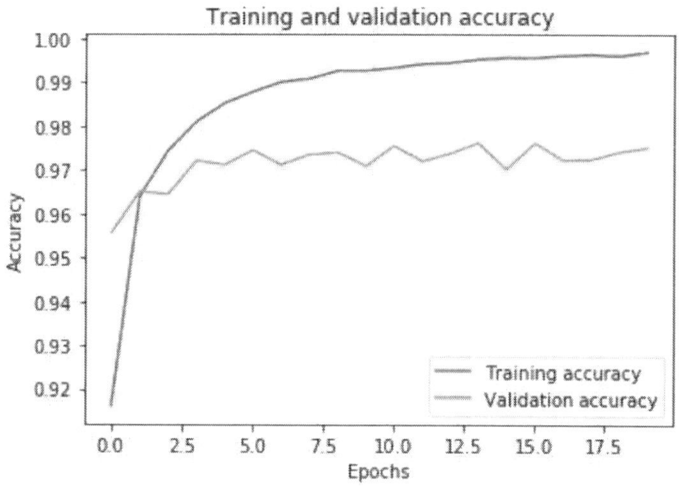

From these plots, we see that we start overfitting slightly after the 2th or 3th epoch, and the validation loss starts creeping up after the 5th epoch. So, we should train this particular model for only 2-6 epochs.

One disadvantage of the history callback is that we can use it only after the entire completion of the training process for the entire number of epochs set in the fit method. However, in addition to the history callback, there are many other useful callbacks in Keras that don't have this disadvantage and that allow greater functionality. For example, there is a callback that allows us to stop training when a certain condition occurs during the training process. This condition may be, for instance, the point when the validation loss is no longer improving. This callback is called **EarlyStopping**.

Also, there is a callback for visualization of a training process that we can use even before completion of training. This callback is called **TensorBoard**. And there is a special browser-based API for this, which is also called TensorBoard and included in TensorFlow. The TensorBoard API is a wonderful tool for tuning deep neural networks. The functionality of this API is much, much richer than the functionality of the history callback.

As I said, the history callback is applied to every model automatically, but if we want to use other callbacks, we need directly specify them in the fit method. For example, here is how it may look like when we use the **EarlyStopping** callback:

```
from tensorflow.keras.callbacks import EarlyStopping

earlystopping = EarlyStopping(monitor='val_loss',
patience=1)

model.fit(partial_x_train, partial_y_train,
validation_data=(x_val, y_val),  epochs=10,
callbacks=[earlystopping])
```

Of course, different callbacks have different parameters, which we can find in the Keras documentation. By the way, we can even build our own callbacks, but it's more advanced material.

Image classification with a convolutional network

So far, we've been building very simple deep neural networks. In this chapter, we will take on constructing a more complex neural network. It's going to be a convolutional network for image classification.

We'll be working with the CIFAR-10 dataset. Like the MNIST dataset, CIFAR-10 is also a very popular dataset for image classification in the machine learning community and available in Keras. This dataset consists of 60.000 32x32 pixel color images belonging to 10 classes with 6,000 images per class (https://www.cs.toronto.edu/~kriz/cifar.html).

As always, first of all, we import all the packages we need:

```
import tensorflow

from tensorflow.keras.datasets import cifar10

from tensorflow.keras.models import Model

from tensorflow.keras.layers import Dense, Flatten, Input

from tensorflow.keras.layers import Dropout, BatchNormalization

from tensorflow.keras.layers import Conv2D, MaxPooling2D
```

```
from tensorflow.keras.preprocessing import image
from tensorflow.keras.optimizers import Adam
from tensorflow.keras.callbacks import EarlyStopping
import matplotlib.pyplot as plt
import numpy as np
 from keras.utils import np_utils
```

Then, we download the dataset,

```
(x_train, y_train), (x_test, y_test) = cifar10.load_data()
```

normalize the data, and convert our dependant vectors into categorical labels:

```
x_train = x_train.astype('float32')
x_test =x_test.astype('float32')
x_train /= 255
x_test /= 255
number_of_classes = 10
```

```
y_train = np_utils.to_categorical(y_train, number_of_classes)

y_test = np_utils.to_categorical(y_test, number_of_classes)
```

Now we're ready to construct the network. Doing this task, I tried a few slightly different architectures and chose one which produced slightly better results. So, hcrc the code:

```
inputs = Input(shape=(32, 32, 3))

x = BatchNormalization()(inputs)

x = Conv2D(32, (3, 3), padding='same', activation='relu')(x)

x = BatchNormalization()(x)

x = Conv2D(32, (3, 3), padding='same', activation='relu')(x)

x = Dropout(0.25)(x)

x = BatchNormalization()(x)

x = Conv2D(32, (3, 3), padding='same', activation='relu')(x)

x = Dropout(0.25)(x)

x = BatchNormalization()(x)

x = Conv2D(32, (3, 3), padding='same', activation='relu')(x)

x = Dropout(0.25)(x)
```

```
x = Conv2D(32, (3, 3), padding='same', activation='relu')(x)
x = MaxPooling2D(pool_size=(2, 2))(x)
x = Dropout(0.25)(x)
x = BatchNormalization()(x)
x = Conv2D(64, (3, 3), padding='same', activation='relu')(x)
x = Dropout(0.25)(x)
x = Conv2D(64, (3, 3), activation='relu')(x)
x = MaxPooling2D(pool_size=(2, 2))(x)
x = Dropout(0.25)(x)
x = Flatten()(x)
x = Dense(512, activation='relu')(x)
x = Dropout(0.5)(x)
outputs = Dense(10, activation='softmax')(x)
model = Model(inputs, outputs)

model.summary()
```

```
_________________________________________________________________
Layer (type)                 Output Shape              Param #
=================================================================
input_11 (InputLayer)        (None, 32, 32, 3)         0
_________________________________________________________________
batch_normalization_57 (Batc (None, 32, 32, 3)         12
_________________________________________________________________
conv2d_72 (Conv2D)           (None, 32, 32, 32)        896
_________________________________________________________________
batch_normalization_58 (Batc (None, 32, 32, 32)        128
_________________________________________________________________
conv2d_73 (Conv2D)           (None, 32, 32, 32)        9248
_________________________________________________________________
dropout_69 (Dropout)         (None, 32, 32, 32)        0
_________________________________________________________________
batch_normalization_59 (Batc (None, 32, 32, 32)        128
_________________________________________________________________
conv2d_74 (Conv2D)           (None, 32, 32, 32)        9248
_________________________________________________________________
dropout_70 (Dropout)         (None, 32, 32, 32)        0
_________________________________________________________________
batch_normalization_60 (Batc (None, 32, 32, 32)        128
_________________________________________________________________
conv2d_75 (Conv2D)           (None, 32, 32, 32)        9248
_________________________________________________________________
dropout_71 (Dropout)         (None, 32, 32, 32)        0
_________________________________________________________________
conv2d_76 (Conv2D)           (None, 32, 32, 32)        9248
_________________________________________________________________
max_pooling2d_20 (MaxPooling (None, 16, 16, 32)        0
_________________________________________________________________
dropout_72 (Dropout)         (None, 16, 16, 32)        0
_________________________________________________________________
batch_normalization_61 (Batc (None, 16, 16, 32)        128
_________________________________________________________________
conv2d_77 (Conv2D)           (None, 16, 16, 64)        18496
_________________________________________________________________
dropout_73 (Dropout)         (None, 16, 16, 64)        0
_________________________________________________________________
conv2d_78 (Conv2D)           (None, 14, 14, 64)        36928
_________________________________________________________________
max_pooling2d_21 (MaxPooling (None, 7, 7, 64)          0
_________________________________________________________________
dropout_74 (Dropout)         (None, 7, 7, 64)          0
_________________________________________________________________
flatten_10 (Flatten)         (None, 3136)              0
_________________________________________________________________
dense_20 (Dense)             (None, 512)               1606144
_________________________________________________________________
dropout_75 (Dropout)         (None, 512)               0
_________________________________________________________________
dense_21 (Dense)             (None, 10)                5130
=================================================================
Total params: 1,705,110
Trainable params: 1,704,848
```

So, it's a convolutional network with seven convolutional layers and with over 1.7 million trainable parameters. We use dropout almost after each layer. We didn't do that in our earlier networks. Also, we use batch normalization in this network.

Let's look at the **Conv2D** method we've used for constructing convolutional layers in our network, for example:

```
Conv2D(32, (3, 3), padding='same', activation='relu')(x)
```

In this method, the first parameter specifies the number of filters in a conv. layer. In the brackets, next to the number of filters, we specified the first two dimensions of these filters. The third dimension of a filter is always equal to the third dimension (the number of channels) of an input, and we don't need to specify it in the code.

By using the **same** attribute for the parameter **padding,** we make a conv. layer output such that this output has the same dimensionality as the input to this layer. In other words, we don't lose the dimensionality of our data samples when we use the "same" attribute.

In this network, we use the Adam algorithm with a slightly reduced learning rate as an optimizer:

```
adam = Adam(lr=0.0005)
```

We compile the network:

```
model.compile(optimizer=adam,
        loss='categorical_crossentropy',
        metrics=['accuracy'])
```

As you can see, in this network, we use the standard types of a loss function and metrics for classification tasks.

Also, in this network, we use the **EarlyStopping** callback:

```
earlystopping = EarlyStopping(monitor='val_acc', patience=3)
```

Now we can call the **fit** method and train this network:

```
model.fit(x_train, y_train, validation_split=0.1,
        shuffle=True, batch_size=32,
```

```
epochs=50, callbacks=[earlystopping])
```

And after training, we evaluate it:

```
model.evaluate(x_test, y_test, verbose=2)
```

```
[0.6015201451778411, 0.7996]
```

This network is not ideal for this task, but having around 80% accuracy is still a pretty decent result.

CIFAR-10 has 10 classes: airplane (0), automobile (1), bird (2), car (3), deer (4), dog (5), frog (6), horse (7), ship (8), and truck (9). In the brackets, I put up their corresponding labels in the dataset.

Having trained the model, we can use it for making predictions on new data, and it's fun.

I prepared a few images to classify with this network:

First of all, we make a dictionary for our labels:

classes = {"0":"Plane", "1":"Car", "2":"Bird", "3":"Cat", "4":"Deer", "5":"Dog", "6" :"Frog", "7" :"Horse", "8" :"Ship", "9" :"Truck"}

Then, in the following code, we take our image of a plane and convert it into a 32x32 image:

img_path = "military-raptor-582888_640.jpg"

img = image.load_img(img_path, target_size=(32,32))

Let's look at this new converted image:

```
plt.imshow(img)

plt.show()
```

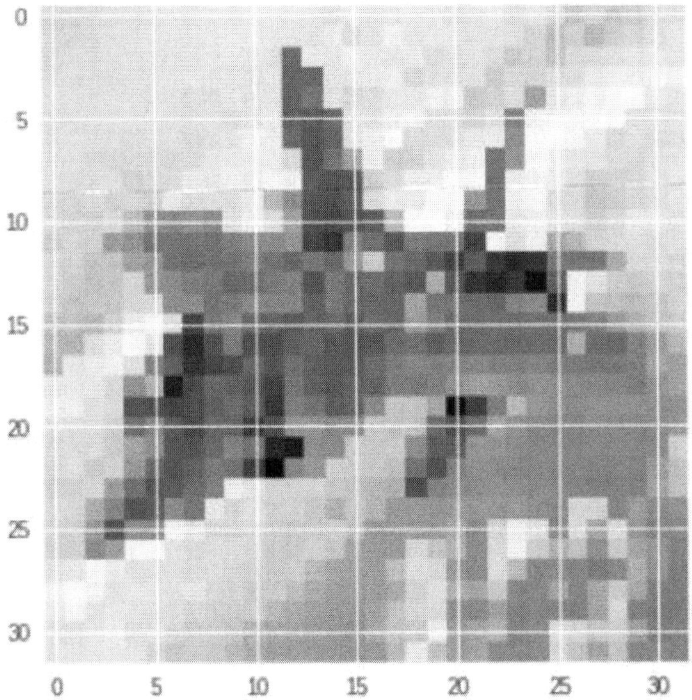

Then, we convert this image into a numpy array and normalize it:

```
x = image.img_to_array(img)

x /= 255

x = np.expand_dims(x, axis=0)
```

Now, we call the predict method:

```
prediction = model.predict(x)

print(prediction)
```

And we see a bunch of scary probabilities:

```
[[9.9816918e-01 2.9563316e-10 3.6799465e-05 7.7521054e-06 1.7750830e-03
  6.0884777e-09 1.0941272e-07 6.1034866e-06 4.9542878e-06 5.4685939e-10]]
```

Now we execute the following code:

```
pr = np.argmax(prediction)

for k,v in classes.items():

    if k == str(pr):

        print("It's a", v)
```

Finally, we obtained the result of our prediction in a readable form:

```
It's a plane
```

So, the network has made a correct prediction on this instance.

Let’s do the same for the image of a car:

```
img_path2 = "car-49278_640.jpg"

img2 = image.load_img(img_path2, target_size=(32,32))

x = image.img_to_array(img2)

x /= 255

x = np.expand_dims(x, axis=0)

prediction = model.predict(x)

pr = np.argmax(prediction)

for k,v in classes.items():

    if k == str(pr):

        print("It's a", v)
```

```
It's a car
```

Again, our network is correct.

Now let's do the same for the image of a horse. But note that this image isn't as straightforward as the previous two.

```
img_path3 = "horses-back-587609_640.jpg"
img3 = image.load_img(img_path3, target_size=(32,32))
x = image.img_to_array(img3)
x /= 255
x = np.expand_dims(x, axis=0)
prediction = model.predict(x)
pr = np.argmax(prediction)
for k,v in classes.items():
    if k == str(pr):
        print("It's a", v)
```

As a result, we get:

```
It's a frog
```

So, the network for some reason thinks that this image of a horse's back is a frog.

I put up the code for this network on my github: https://github.com/ArtemKovera/deeplearning/blob/classification/cifar10_conv.ipynb

More my Books

If you like this book, you can also check out other my books:

Machine Learning with Clustering: A Visual Guide with Examples in Python

How to Create Machine Superintelligence: A Quick Journey through Classical/Quantum Computing, Artificial Intelligence, Machine Learning, and Neural Networks (Second Edition)

Thank You for Buying my Books!!!

References and some other useful resources on deep learning

Sandro Skansi. *Introduction to Deep Learning: From Logical Calculus to Artificial Intelligence (Undergraduate Topics in Computer Science)*, 2018

Francois Chollet. *Deep Learning with Python*, 2018

Mike Bernico. *Deep Learning Quick Reference. Useful hacks for training and optimizing deep neural networks with TensorFlow and Keras*, 2018

Armando Vieira, Bernardete Ribeiro. *Introduction to Deep Learning Business Applications for Developers: From Conversational Bots in Customer Service to Medical Image Processing*, 2018

Dipanjan Sarkar, Raghav Bali, Tamoghna Ghosh. *Hands-On Transfer Learning with Python: Implement advanced deep learning and neural network models using TensorFlow and Keras*, 2018

Ian Goodfellow, Yoshua Bengio, Aaron Courville. *Deep learning (adaptive computation and machine learning series)*, 2016 (https://www.deeplearningbook.org/)

Richard S. Sutton and Andrew G. Barto. *Reinforcement Learning: An Introduction* (Second edition, in progress), 2014-2017 (http://incompleteideas.net/book/bookdraft2017nov5.pdf)

Sebastian Ruder. *An overview of gradient descent optimization algorithms*, 2016

(https://arxiv.org/abs/1609.04747, also at http://ruder.io/optimizing-gradient-descent/)

Christian Szegedy, Wei Liu, Yangqing Jia, Pierre Sermanet, Scott Reed, Dragomir Anguelov, Dumitru Erhan, Vincent Vanhoucke, Andrew Rabinovich. Going Deeper with Convolutions, 2014 (https://arxiv.org/abs/1409.4842)

Kaiming He, Xiangyu Zhang, Shaoqing Ren, Jian Sun. Deep Residual Learning for Image Recognition, 2015 (https://arxiv.org/abs/1512.03385)

Diederik P. Kingma, Jimmy Ba. Adam: A Method for Stochastic Optimization, 2013 (https://arxiv.org/abs/1412.6980)

Gamaleldin F. Elsayed, Ian Goodfellow, Jascha Sohl-Dickstein. *Adversarial Reprogramming of Neural Networks*, 2018 (https://arxiv.org/abs/1806.11146)

Andrei A. Rusu, Neil C. Rabinowitz, Guillaume Desjardins, Hubert Soyer, James Kirkpatrick, Koray Kavukcuoglu, Razvan Pascanu, Raia Hadsell. *Progressive Neural Networks*, 2016 (https://arxiv.org/abs/1606.04671)

Felipe Petroski Such, Vashisht Madhavan, Edoardo Conti, Joel Lehman, Kenneth O. Stanley, Jeff Clune. *Deep Neuroevolution: Genetic Algorithms Area Competitive Alternative for Training Deep Neural Networks for Reinforcement Learning*, 2017 (https://arxiv.org/abs/1712.06567)

Ian J. Goodfellow, Jean Pouget-Abadie, Mehdi Mirza, Bing Xu, David Warde-Farley, Sherjil Ozair, Aaron Courville, Yoshua Bengio. *Generative Adversarial Networks*, 2014 (https://arxiv.org/abs/1406.2661)

Volodymyr Mnih, Koray Kavukcuoglu, David Silver, Alex Graves, Ioannis Antonoglou, Daan Wierstra, Martin Riedmiller. *Playing Atari with Deep Reinforcement Learning*, 2013 (https://arxiv.org/abs/1312.5602)

David Silver, Aja Huang, Chris J. Maddison, Arthur Guez, Laurent Sifre, George van den Driessche, Julian Schrittwieser, Ioannis Antonoglou, Veda Panneershelvam, Marc Lanctot, Sander Dieleman, Dominik Grewe, John Nham, Nal Kalchbrenner, Ilya Sutskever, Timothy Lillicrap, Madeleine Leach, Koray Kavukcuoglu, Thore Graepel & Demis Hassabis. *Mastering the game of Go with deep neural networks and tree search*, 2016 (https://www.nature.com/articles/nature16961)

David Silver, Julian Schrittwieser, Karen Simonyan, Ioannis Antonoglou, Aja Huang, Arthur Guez, Thomas Hubert, Lucas Baker, Matthew Lai, Adrian Bolton, Yutian Chen, Timothy Lillicrap, Fan Hui, Laurent Sifre, George van den Driessche, Thore Graepel & Demis Hassabis. *Mastering the game of Go without human knowledge*, 2017 (https://www.nature.com/articles/nature24270)

https://www.deeplearning.ai – Andrew Ng's courses

http://videolectures.net/eml07_lecun_wia/ – Yann LeCun's lecture "Who Is Afraid of Non-Convex Functions?"

http://videolectures.net/rldm2015_silver_reinforcement_learning/ David Silver's introductory lecture on deep reinforcement learning

https://www.youtube.com/watch?v=60xbDEpA49M Andrey Sozykin's tutorial on TPU Google Colaboratory (It's in Russian) https://www.youtube.com/watch?v=RznKVRTFkBY&list=PLZbbT5o_s2xrwRnXk_yCPtnqqo4_u2YGL – good playlist on Keras from Deeplizard

https://towardsdatascience.com

https://machinelearningmastery.com

http://neuralnetworksanddeeplearning.com/

https://cloud.google.com/tpu/docs/tpus – Google TPU documentation

42560043R00119

Printed in Poland
by Amazon Fulfillment
Poland Sp. z o.o., Wrocław